THE
★ ALL- ★
AMERICAN
QUOTE BOOK

Michael Reagan
AND
BOB PHILLIPS

HARVEST HOUSE PUBLISHERS
Eugene, Oregon 97402

THE ALL-AMERICAN QUOTE BOOK

Copyright © 1995 by Harvest House Publishers
Eugene, Oregon 97402

Library of Congress Cataloging-in-Publication Data

The all-American quote book / (compiled by) Michael
  Reagan & Bob Phillips.
      p.   cm.
    ISBN 1-56507-346-0
    1. Quotations, English. 2. Spiritual life—Christianity—
Quotations, maxims, etc.   I. Reagan, Michael, 1945–
II. Phillips, Bob, 1940–
PN6084.R3A54   1995
081—dc20   94-48344
                                                       CIP

Printed in the United States of America.

     96 97 98 99 00 — 10 9 8 7 6 5 4

CONTENTS
★ A-Z ★

ABILITY

Behind an able man there are always
other able men.

There is something that is much scarcer,
something finer by far, something rarer than
ability. It is the ability to recognize ability.

Elbert Hubbard

We judge ourselves by what we feel capable
of doing, while others judge us by what we
have already done.

Henry Wadsworth Longfellow

The winds and waves are always on the
side of the ablest navigators.

Edward Gibbon

Ability is of little account without opportunity.

Napoleon Bonaparte

Neglect not the gift that is in thee.
The Bible

You can always tell luck from ability by its duration.

ABSENCE

If your absence won't make any difference,
your presence won't either. Absence makes
the heart grow fonder.
Thomas Haynes Bayly

ACCEPTANCE

He who doesn't accept the conditions
of life sells his soul.
Charles Baudelaire

When we have accepted the worst, we have
nothing more to lose. And that automatically
means—we have everything to gain.
Dale Carnegie

ACCOMPLISHMENT

No matter what your lot in life, build
something on it.

Lord, grant that I may always desire more
than I can accomplish.
Michelangelo

ACHIEVEMENT

If you want a place in the sun, you will have
to expect some blisters.

He who wants to get
to the top must get off his bottom.

ACQUAINTANCE

Acquaintance: a person whom we know
well enough to borrow from, but not well
enough to lend to.

Ambrose Bierce

ACTION

To put your ideas into action is the most
difficult thing in the world.

Johann Wolfgang von Goethe

Action may not always bring happiness; but
there is no happiness without action.

Benjamin Disraeli

If the wind will not serve, take to the oars.

ACTORS

You can pick out actors by the glazed look
that comes to their eyes when the conversation
wanders away from themselves.

ADAPTABILITY

We must make the best of those ills which
cannot be avoided.

Alexander Hamilton

ADMIRE

We always admire the other fellow more after
we have tried to do his job.

William C. Feather

We always like those who admire us, but we do
not always like those whom we admire.

Francois de La Rochefoucauld

ADOLESCENCE

Adolescence is like a hitch in the Army—you'd hate to
have missed it, and yet you'd hate to repeat it.

Don't bite the hand that has your allowance in it.

Paul Dickson

ADULTERY

But the man who commits adultery is an utter
fool, for he destroys his own soul.

The Bible

In every affair consider what precedes
and what follows.

Epictetus

Can a man hold fire against his chest
and not be burned?

The Bible

ADVERSARY

Next to a happy family and a few good friends,
the best human gift that God can give to any
man is a worthy adversary.

ADVERSITY

You are a poor specimen if you can't stand the
pressure of adversity.

The Bible

Adversity causes some men to break; others
to break records.

William A. Ward

Prosperity is a great teacher; adversity is a
greater. Possession pampers the mind; privation
trains and strengthens it.

William Hazlitt

Adversity makes men think of God.

Livy

In time of prosperity friends will be plenty;
In times of adversity not one in twenty.

The bravest sight in all this world is a man
fighting against odds.

Franklin K. Lane

Kites rise highest against the wind—not with it.

Winston Churchill

Discover someone to help shoulder your misfortunes.
Then you will never be alone . . . neither fate, nor the
crowd, so readily attacks two.

Baltasar Gracian

There is in every true woman's heart a spark
of heavenly fire, which lies dormant in the broad day-
light of prosperity; but which kindles up, and beams
and blazes in the dark hour of adversity.

Washington Irving

Adversity introduces a man to himself.

God brings men into deep waters, not to
drown them, but to cleanse them.

Aughey

ADVERTISING

When business is good, it pays to advertise; when
business is bad, you've got to advertise.

Of the ninety percent of businesses that fail,
they fail in the area of advertising.

Doing business without advertising is like winking
at a girl in the dark: You know what you are
doing but nobody else does.

Ed Howe

ADVICE

How is it possible to expect mankind
to take advice when they will not so
much as take warning?

Jonathan Swift

Get all the advice you can and be wise the
rest of your life.

The Bible

Timely advice is as lovely as gold apples
in a silver basket.

The Bible

We give advice by the bucket, but take it by the grain.

W. R. Alger

Admonish your friends privately,
but praise them openly.

Publilius Syrus

When a man comes to me for advice, I find out the
kind of advice he wants—and I give it to him.

Josh Billings

A good scare is worth more to a man
than good advice.

Watson Edger Howe

Advice for a teenage daughter—five inexpensive
beauty hints: For attractive lips, speak words of kindness; For lovely eyes, seek out the good in people;
For a slim figure, share your food with the hungry;
For beautiful hair, let a child run his fingers through it
once a day. And, for poise, walk with the knowledge
that you will never walk alone.

Sam Levenson

I realize that advice is worth what it
costs—that is, nothing.

Douglas MacArthur

Some folks won't ask for advice for fear of giving the impression they need it.

AFFECTIONS

Above all else, guard your affections. For they influence everything else in your life.

The Bible

AGE

It takes about ten years to get used to how old you are. I am not young enough to know everything.

Oscar Wilde

The ten best years of a woman's life are between the ages of twenty-nine and thirty.

Peter Weiss

Age does not protect you from love. But love, to some extent, protects you from age.

He who is of a calm and happy nature will hardly feel the pressure of age, but to him who is of an opposite disposition youth and age are equally a burden.

Plato

AGREEABLE

My idea of an agreeable person is a person who agrees with me.

Benjamin Disraeli

If you wish to appear agreeable in society,
you must consent to be taught many things
which you know already.

Charles Maurice de Talleyrand

Nobody can be as agreeable as an
uninvited guest.

Kin Hubbard

AILMENTS

For every ailment under the sun, there is a remedy, or
there is none; if there be one, try to find it;
if there be none, never mind it.

We are so fond of one another because our
ailments are the same.

Jonathan Swift

AIRLINES

You can't fool all the people all the time, but the air-
plane schedules come pretty close.

ALARM CLOCK

An alarm clock is a device for awakening people
who don't have small children.

ALCOHOL

Alcohol is used by a majority of the adult
population and creates more problems than all
other drugs combined.

Robert Elliott

★ 19 ★

ALONE

The human race is not alone in the
universe . . . . I am not alone.
Richard E. Byrd

AMBITION

Ambition and death are alike in this:
neither is ever satisfied.
The Bible

By working faithfully eight hours a day
you may eventually get to be a boss and
work twelve hours a day.
Robert Frost

There was a kid on the block who always
wanted to be a pirate when he grew up. Today
he is a doctor. He's lucky. Not every man realizes
the ambitions of his youth.

I . . . had ambition not only to go farther than any
man had ever been before, but as far as it was
possible for a man to go.
Captain James Cook

A man of high ambitions must leave even
his fellow adventurers and go forth into
deeper solitude and greater trials.

AMERICA

I only regret that I have but one life
to lose for my country.
Nathan Hale

Americans are like a rich father who wishes he knew how to give his son the hardships that made him rich.

Robert Frost

The things that will destroy America are prosperity-at-any-price, safety-first instead of duty-first, the love of soft living, and the get-rich-quick theory of life.

Theodore Roosevelt

Indeed, I tremble for my country when I reflect that God is just.

Thomas Jefferson

The first requisite of a good citizen in this republic of ours is that he shall be able and willing to pull his weight.

Theodore Roosevelt

My God! How little do my countrymen know what precious blessings they are in possession of, and which no other people on earth enjoy!

Thomas Jefferson

The fabulous country—the place where miracles not only happen, but where they happen all the time.

Thomas Wolfe

There is nothing wrong with America that the faith, love of freedom, intelligence, and energy of her citizens can not cure.

Dwight D. Eisenhower

The winds that blow through the wide sky in these mountains, the winds that sweep from Canada to Mexico, from the Pacific to the

Atlantic—have always
blown on free men.
Franklin D. Roosevelt

There is nothing wrong with America that
together we can't fix.
Ronald Reagan

If we do not make a common cause to save the good
old ship of the Union on this voyage, nobody will
have a chance to pilot her on another voyage.
Abraham Lincoln

And so, my fellow Americans: Ask not what your
country can do for you—ask what you can do for
your country. My fellow citizens of the world: Ask
not what America will do for you, but what together
we can do for the freedom of man.
John F. Kennedy

The only foes that threaten America are the
enemies at home, and these are ignorance,
superstition, and incompetence.
Elbert Hubbard

America is the only country in the world
where a man can afford to build a four-bedroom
house by the time all of his children are old enough
to go to college.

This is America . . . a brilliant diversity spread
like stars, like a thousand points of light in a
broad and peaceful sky.
George Bush

America is still the land of opportunity. Where
else could you earn enough to owe so much?

America is too great for
small dreams.
Ronald Reagan

The modern American drives a bank-financed
car over a bond-financed highway on credit-card
gas to open a charge account at a department
store so he can fill his savings-and-loan-financed
home with installment-purchased furniture.

The Europeans were delighted when
Christopher Columbus discovered
America. At last they had somewhere
to borrow money from.

I am tired of hearing that democracy doesn't
work—it isn't supposed to work. We
are supposed to work it.
Alexander Woolcott

There is no room in this country for hyphenated
Americans. . . . The one absolutely certain
way of bringing this nation to ruin, of
preventing all possibility of continuing to
be a nation at all would be to permit it to
become a tangle of squabbling nationalities.
Theodore Roosevelt

Recognition of the Supreme Being is the first, the
most basic, expression of Americanism. Without
God, there could be no American form of
government, nor American way of life.
Dwight D. Eisenhower

I don't think it does any harm just once in a
while to acknowledge that the whole country
isn't in flames, that there are people in the

country besides politicians,
entertainers, and criminals.

Charles Kuralt

America is a tune. It must be sung together.

Gerald Stanley Lee

America is a large friendly dog in a small
room. Every time it wags its tail
it knocks over a chair.

Arnold Toynbee

That's America for you. They won't let kids pray in
school, but they put Bibles in prisons.

Double—no triple—our troubles and we'd
still be better off than any other people on earth.

Ronald Reagan

There can be no fifty-fifty Americanism in this
country. There is room here for only
hundred-percent Americanism.

Theodore Roosevelt

"Keep, ancient lands, your storied pomp!"
cries she with silent lips. "Give me your tired,
your poor, your huddled masses yearning to breathe
free, the wretched refuse of your teeming shore.
Send these, the homeless, tempest-tossed, to me;
I lift my lamp beside the golden door.

Emma Lazarus

If America ever passes out as a great nation, we
ought to put on our tombstone: America died from a
delusion she had Moral Leadership.

Will Rogers

ANCESTRY

I don't know who my grandfather was; I am much
more concerned to know what his grandson will be.

Abraham Lincoln

ANGELS

Man was created a little lower than the angels, and
has been getting a little lower ever since.

Mark Twain

ANGER

Anger is just one letter short of danger.

Anger is quieted by a gentle word, just as
fire is quenched by water.

Keep away from angry, short-tempered men, lest you
learn to be like them and endanger your soul.

The Bible

When angry, count to ten before you speak: if
very angry, a hundred.

Thomas Jefferson

The greatest cure of anger is delay.

Seneca

No man can think clearly when his fists are clenched.

George Jean Nathan

ANIMALS

The animals are not as stupid as one thinks—they
have neither doctors nor lawyers.

L. Docquier

ANOREXIA

Where do you go to get anorexia?

Shelley Winters

ANSWER

A gentle answer turns away wrath, but harsh words
cause quarrels.

The Bible

If a gentle answer turns away wrath, not using gentle
words will turn wrath your way.

No answer is also an answer.

ANT

None preaches better than the ant,
and she says nothing.

Benjamin Franklin

ANXIETY

Up to a certain point anxiety is good, for it promotes
action. Beyond that point we freeze any fixed
attitudes or rush about without thinking deeply
from one decision to another.

Jules Henry

Borrow trouble for yourself, if that's your nature, but don't lend it to your neighbors.

Rudyard Kipling

APATHY

Science may have found a cure for most evils; but it has found no remedy for the worst of them all—the apathy of human beings.

Helen Keller

All that is necessary for the forces of evil to win in the world is for enough good men to do nothing.

Edmund Burke

APPEARANCES

Appearances deceive and this one maxim is a standing rule: Men are not what they seem.

Never suffer your courage to exert itself in fierceness, your resolution in obstinacy, your wisdom in cunning, nor your patience in sullenness and despair.

Charles Palmer

APPRECIATION

I would rather appreciate the things I do not have than to have things I do not appreciate.

By appreciation we make excellence in others our own property.

Voltaire

The deepest principle in human nature
is the craving to be appreciated.

William James

You can't appreciate home till you've left it, money till
it's spent, your wife till she's joined a woman's club,
and Old Glory till you see it hanging on a broom stick
of a counsul in a foreign town.

O. Henry

ARCHITECTURE

Architecture is frozen music.

Johann Wolfgang von Goethe

ARGUE

There's nothing so annoying as arguing with a person
who knows what he is talking about.

Some arguments are sound, and nothing more.

Richard Armour

Arguing is a game that two can play at. But it is a
strange game in that neither opponent ever wins.

Benjamin Franklin

I always get the better when I argue alone.

Oliver Goldsmith

Never make the mistake of arguing with people for
whose opinions you have no respect.

A dry crust eaten in peace is better than steak every
day along with argument and strife.

The Bible

ART

Nothing is so poor and melancholy as art that is interested in itself and not in its subject.

George Santayana

ATHEIST

The worst moment for the atheist is when he is really thankful and has nobody to thank.

Dante Gabriel Rossetti

Did you hear about the "Dial A Prayer" for atheists? You dial a number and no one answers.

I was going to be an atheist, but I gave it up. They don't have any holidays.

An atheist does not find God for the same reason a thief does not find a policeman.

ATTITUDE

Things are for us only what we hold them to be. Which is to say that our attitude toward things is more likely in the long run to be more important than the things themselves.

A. W. Tozer

When a man is gloomy, everything seems to go wrong; when he is cheerful, everything seems right!

The Bible

Don't bother to give God instructions; just report for duty.

Corrie Ten Boom

Be like a duck—keep calm and unruffled on
the surface, but paddle like crazy underneath.

Assume a cheerfulness you do not
feel and shortly you will feel the
cheerfulness you assumed.

I am more and more convinced that
our happiness or unhappiness depends far more
on the way we meet the events of life than on the
nature of those events themselves.

Wilhelm Von Humboldt

To look up and not down,
To look forward and not back,
To look out and not in, and
To lend a hand.

Edward Everett Hale

Two men look out through the same bars;
One sees the mud, and one the stars . . .

Frederick Langbridge

When life gives you lemons, make lemonade.

Our life is what our thoughts make it.

Marcus Aurelius

Keep your face to the sunshine and you
cannot see the shadow.

Helen Keller

One man gets nothing but discord out of a piano;
another gets harmony. No one claims the piano is at
fault. Life is about the same. The discord is there,

and the harmony is there. Study to play it correctly, and it will give forth the beauty; play it falsely, and it will give forth the ugliness. Life is not at fault.

If you wish to travel far and fast,
travel light. Take off all your envies, jealousies, unforgiveness, selfishness, and fears.

Glenn Clark

In War: Resolution. In Defeat: Defiance. In Victory: Magnanimity. In Peace: Goodwill.

Winston Churchill

When I hear somebody sigh that "Life is hard," I am always tempted to ask, "Compared to what?"

Sydney Harris

If you've made up your mind that you can't do something—you're absolutely right!

Not knowing when the dawn will come
I open every door.

Emily Dickinson

Things turn out best for people who make the best of the way things turn out.

ATTRIBUTES

Among the attributes of God, although they are all equal, mercy shines with even more brilliancy than justice.

Cervantes

AUTHORITY

Nothing more impairs authority than a too
frequent or indiscreet use of it. If thunder itself
was to be continual, it would excite no more
terror than the noise of a mill.

AUTOMOBILE

The worst kind of car trouble is when the
engine won't start and the payments
won't stop.

Any car will last a lifetime, if you're
careless enough.

AVAILABILITY

God does not ask your ability or your inability. He
asks only your availability.

Mary Kay Ash

AVARICE

If you wish to remove avarice you must
remove its mother, luxury.

Cicero

AVERAGE

If at first you don't succeed, you're about average.

Robert Anthony

BABIES

Babies don't need a traditional slap on the rear end when they are born. But at least it gives them an immediate idea of what life is going to be like.

Out of the mouth of babes comes a lot of what they should have swallowed.

Franklin P. Jones

BACHELOR

A bachelor is a man who can take a nap on top of a bedspread.

Marcelene Cox

BALD

When God made heads, He covered up the ones He didn't like.

BALLOT

The ballot is stronger than the bullet.
Abraham Lincoln

BAR

The best side of a bar is outside.

BARBARIAN

History teaches us that when a barbarian race
confronts a sleeping culture, the barbarian
always wins.
Arnold Toynbee

BARGAIN

One of the difficult tasks in this world is to convince a
woman that even a bargain costs money.
Edgar Watson Howe

It's just as unpleasant to get more than you
bargain for as to get less.
George Bernard Shaw

BEAUTY

Nothing is more beautiful than cheerfulness
in an old face.
J. P. Richter

There is no cosmetic for beauty like happiness.
Lady Blessington

A thing of beauty is a joy forever.
Keats

I don't think of all the misery, but of the beauty that
still remains. . . . My advice is: Go outside, to the
fields, enjoy nature and the sunshine, go out and try
to recapture happiness in yourself and in God.
Think of all the beauty that's still left in and
around you and be happy!
Anne Frank

Beauty is altogether in the eye of the beholder.
Lew Wallace

BEHAVIOR

Be pleasant until ten o'clock in the morning and the
rest of the day will take care of itself.
Elbert Hubbard

BEGINNING

Begin to weave and God will give the thread.

Things are always at their best in their beginning.
Blaise Pascal

BELIEF

What we believe about God is the most
important thing about us.
A. W. Tozer

Believe only half of what you see and
nothing that you hear.
Dinah Mulock Craik

BENEFIT

He who receives a benefit should never forget it; he
who bestows one should never remember it.

Charron

BIBLE

When you have read the Bible, you will know it is
the word of God, because you will have found it the
key to your own heart, your own happiness,
and your own duty.

Woodrow Wilson

A knowledge of the Bible without a college degree is
far more valuable than a college degree without the
knowledge of the Bible.

William Lyon Phelps

The Scriptures teach us the best way of living,
the noblest way of suffering, and the
most comfortable way of dying.

Flavel

Men do not reject the Bible because it contradicts
itself but because it contradicts them.

E. Paul Hovey

If a man's Bible is coming apart, it is an indication that
he himself is fairly well put together.

James Jennings

Why is it that our kids can't read a Bible in school,
but they can in prison?

The Bible will keep you from sin,
or sin will keep you from the Bible.

D. L. Moody

It ain't those parts of the Bible that I can't understand
that bother me, it is the parts that I do understand.

Mark Twain

BIRD

A bird in the hand may soil your sleeve, but as long
as you have got the bird in there, you don't have to
worry about where your next meal is coming from.

Fred Allen

A bird in the hand is worth two in the bush.

Cervantes

Birds of a feather will flock together.

Minsheu

BIRTH

This day shall change all griefs and quarrels into love.

William Shakespeare

The only time a woman wishes she were a year
older is when she is expecting a baby.

BITTERNESS

Bitterness and resentment are conditions of the heart
which develop because a person allows an offense
or disappointment to take root and grow

until it affects his thoughts, actions, and
his interpersonal relationships.

Billy Graham

BLAME

The only person who cannot be helped is that
person who blames others.

Carl Rogers

The quickest way to take the starch out of a fellow
who is always blaming himself is to agree with him.

Josh Billings

To err is human. To blame it on the other guy
is even more human.

Take your life in your own hands, and what
happens? A terrible thing: no one to blame.

Erica Jong

BLESSING

If it is more blessed to give than to receive,
then most of us are content to let the other
fellow have the greater blessing.

Shailer Mathews

BLUFF

The hardest tumble a man can make is to
fall over his own bluff.

Ambrose Bierce

BOAST

Great boaster, little doer.

First do it, then say it.

BOOK

A book is the only place in which you can examine a fragile thought without breaking it, or explore an explosive idea without fear it will go off in your face. . . . It is one of the few havens remaining where a man's mind can get both provocation and privacy.

Edward P. Morgan

The man who doesn't read good books has no advantage over the man who can't read them.

Mark Twain

In every fat book there is a thin book trying to get out.

This book fills a much-needed gap.

Moses Hadas

'Tis pleasant, sure, to see one's name in print; books serve to show a man that those original thoughts of his aren't very new after all.

Lord Byron

There is more treasure in books than in all the pirates' loot on Treasure Island . . . and best of all, you can enjoy these riches every day of your life.

Walt Disney

When I get a little money, I buy books;
and if any is left, I buy food and clothes.

Desiderius Erasmus

No furniture so charming as books, even if you never
open them, or read a single word.

Sydney Smith

The books that everybody admires are
those that nobody reads.

Anatole France

Books are the quietest and most constant of friends;
they are the most accessible and wisest of
counselors, and the most patient of teachers.

Charles W. Eliot

Just the knowledge that a good book is waiting one at
the end of a long day makes that day happier.

Kathleen Norris

There are books of which the backs and covers are
by far the best parts.

Charles Dickens

It is chiefly through books that we enjoy intercourse
with superior minds. . . . In the best books, great men
talk to us, give us their most precious thoughts, and
pour their souls into ours.

William Ellery Channing

Books are the compasses and telescopes and
sextants and charts which other men have prepared
to help us navigate the dangerous seas of human life.

Jesse Lee Bennett

The books which help you most are those which make you think the most.

Theodore Parker

BORE

The secret of being a bore is to tell everything.

Voltaire

A bore is a fellow talker who can change the subject to his topic of conversation faster than you can change it back to yours.

Laurence J. Peter

BOREDOM

It is not the fast tempo of modern life that kills but the boredom, a lack of strong interest, and a failure to grow that destroy. It is the feeling that nothing is worthwhile that makes men ill and unhappy.

Harold Dodds

Millions long for immortality who do not know what to do with themselves on a rainy Sunday afternoon.

Susan Ertz

The most bored people in life are not the underprivileged but the overprivileged.

Fulton Sheen

BORING

I spent a year in that town, one Sunday.

Warwick Deeping

Some people are so boring that they make you waste
an entire day in five minutes.

Jules Renard

BORROWING

He that goes a borrowing goes a sorrowing.

BOSS

The question, "Who ought to be boss?" is like asking,
"Who ought to be the tenor in the quartet?" Obviously,
the man who can sing tenor.

Henry Ford

The people who have the most demanding bosses
are those who are self-employed.

BRAGGING

Nobody's so apt to be a soloist as the fellow who
blows his own horn.

Franklin P. Jones

BRAIN

The brain is a wonderful organ; it starts working the
moment you get up in the morning and does not stop
until you get to the office.

Robert Frost

What's on your mind? If you will
forgive the overstatement.

Fred Allen

BRAVE

Tell a man he is brave, and you help
him to become so.

Thomas Carlyle

It is easy to be brave from a safe distance.

Aesop

Bravery is the capacity to perform properly even
when scared half to death.

General Omar Bradley

To believe yourself brave is to be brave; it is the one
only essential thing.

Joan of Arc

Physical bravery is an animal instinct; moral bravery
is a much higher and truer courage.

Wendell Phillips

BREVITY

It is when I am struggling to be brief
that I become unintelligible.

Horace

Hubert, to be eternal you don't have to be endless.

Muriel Humphrey

BRIDE

The weeping bride makes a laughing wife.

BROKENNESS

A cheerful heart does good like a medicine, but a broken spirit makes one sick.

The Bible

A man's courage can sustain his broken body, but when courage dies, what hope is left?

The Bible

BROTHERHOOD

Be kindly affectioned to one another with brotherly love; in honor preferring one another.

The Bible

If we are not our brother's keeper, let us at least not be his executioner.

Marlon Brando

BURDEN

No one is useless in this world who lightens the burdens of another.

Charles Dickens

It has been well said that no man ever sank under the burden of the day. It is when tomorrow's burden is added to the burden of today that the weight is more than a man can bear.

George MacDonald

BUREAUCRACY

The longer the title, the less important the job.

George McGovern

Bureaucracy defends the status quo long past
time when the quo has lost its status.
Laurence J. Peter

Bureaucrats are the only people in the world
who can say absolutely nothing and mean it.
Hugh Sidey

BUSINESS

An empty stable stays clean—but there is no
income from an empty stable.
The Bible

Any enterprise is built by wise planning,
becomes strong through common sense, and
profits wonderfully by keeping abreast of the facts.
The Bible

Develop your business first before
building your house.
The Bible

No nation was ever ruined by trade.
Benjamin Franklin

Whenever you see a successful business, someone
once made a courageous decision.
Peter Drucker

One man's wage rise is another man's price increase.
Harold Wilson

Meetings are indispensable when you
don't want to do anything.
J. K. Galbraith

Invest in inflation. It's the only thing going up.

Will Rogers

A company is judged by the president it keeps.

James Hulbert

Along this tree from root to crown
Ideas flow up and vetoes down.

Peter Drucker

The man who minds his own business usually
has a good one.

In the end, all business operations can be reduced to
three words: people, product, and profits.
People come first.

Lee Iacocca

It either is or ought to be evident to everyone that
business has to prosper before anybody
can get any benefit from it.

Theodore Roosevelt

One great cause of failure of young
men in business is the lack
of concentration.

Andrew Carnegie

A man without a smiling face must not open a shop.

BUSY

We are always too busy for our children; we
never give them the time or interest they deserve.
We lavish gifts upon them; but the most precious

gift—our personal association, which means so much to them—we give grudgingly.

Mark Twain

CALAMITY

Calamities are of two kinds: misfortune to ourselves, and good fortune to others.

Ambrose Bierce

CALM

Be calm in arguing; for fierceness makes error a fault, and truth discourtesy; calmness is a great advantage.

George Herbert

CANDOR

Candor is always a double-edged sword; it may heal or it may separate.

Dr. Wilhelm Stekel

The art of life is to show your hand. There is no diplomacy like candor. You may lose by it now and

then, but it will be a loss well gained if you do.
Nothing is so boring as having to
keep up a deception.

E. V. Lucas

CAPITALISM

The inherent vice of capitalism is the unequal sharing
of blessings; the inherent vice of socialism is the
equal sharing of miseries.

Winston Churchill

Capitalism and communism stand at opposite
poles. Their essential difference is this: The
communist, seeing the rich man and his
fine home says: "No man should have so
much." The capitalist, seeing the same thing,
says: "All men should have as much."

Phelps Adams

Capitalism is the best means ever found to
motivate men.

The capitalist system does not
guarantee that everybody will become
rich, but it guarantees that
anybody can become rich.

Raul R. de Sales

CARE

If you think nobody cares if you're alive, try missing
a couple of car payments.

Earl Wilson

A good manager is a man who isn't worried about his
own career but rather the careers of those who work

for him. My advice: Don't worry about yourself. Take care of those who work for you and you'll float to greatness on their achievements.

H. M. S. Burns

Nobody cares how much you know—until they know how much you care.

John Cassis

To carry care to bed is to sleep with a pack on your back.

Haliburton

CARELESSNESS

For want of a nail the shoe was lost; for want of a shoe the horse was lost; and for the want of a horse the rider was lost; being overtaken and slain by the enemy, all for want of care about a horseshoe nail.

Benjamin Franklin

CAREER

Start planning your second career while you're still on your first one.

David Brown

CATS

No matter how much cats fight, there always seem to be plenty of kittens.

Abraham Lincoln

When the cat's away the mice will play.

James Russell Lowell

CAUTION

Don't throw away the old bucket until you know
whether the new one holds water.

It is a good thing to learn caution by the
misfortunes of others.
Publilius Syrus

Just because the river is quiet, don't think the
crocodiles have left.

Little boats should keep near shore.
Benjamin Franklin

There's always free cheese
in a mousetrap.

CELEBRITY

A celebrity is a person who works hard all his life to
become well known, and then wears dark glasses to
avoid being recognized.
Fred Allen

CHALLENGE

Challenge causes one to rise to the occasion and put
forth his best abilities to overcome obstacles and
pressures and grow in character.

Do the hard jobs first. The easy jobs will take
care of themselves.
Dale Carnegie

CHANGE

All change represents loss of some kind; that's why
some of us resist it so strongly.

Consider how hard it is to change yourself
and you'll understand what little chance you have
of trying to change others.

Jacob M. Braude

Change is always hard for the man who is in a rut.
For he has scaled down his living to that which he
can handle comfortably and welcomes no change—
or challenge—that would lift him.

C. Neil Strait

The world hates change; yet it is the only
thing that has brought progress.

Charles Kettering

CHARACTER

Ability will enable a man to get to the top, but it
takes character to keep him there.

If I keep my good character, I shall be rich enough.

Platonicus

A person reveals his character by nothing so
clearly as the joke he resents.

George Christoph Lichtenberg

You can tell a company by the men it keeps.

W. A. Clarke

A man can be no bigger than the number of people
for whom he genuinely cares.

Sherm Williams

Character is what you are in the dark.

D. L. Moody

The way to find out about one man, I have often
found, is to ask him about another.

Gerard Fay

There is nothing so fatal to character as
half-finished tasks.

David Lloyd George

One can acquire everything in solitude—
except character.

Henri Beyle

When the character of a man is not clear to you,
look at his friends.

Character builds slowly, but it can be torn down
with incredible swiftness.

Faith Baldwin

The best index to a person's character is
how he treats people who can't do him
any good, and how he treats people
who can't fight back.

Abigail Van Buren

Houses reveal character.

Gilbert Highet

CHARM

There's a difference between beauty and charm.
A beautiful woman is one I notice. A charming
woman is one who notices me.

John Erskine

If a person has charm he never loses it;
and charm never fatigues.

Andre Maurois

CHEAT

He who will cheat you at play will cheat
you in other ways.

CHEERFUL

I am still determined to be cheerful and happy
in whatever situation I may be, for I have
also learned from experience that the greater
part of our happiness or misery depends on our
dispositions and not on our circumstances.

Martha Washington

You find yourself refreshed by the presence of
cheerful people. Why not make an honest effort to
confer that pleasure on others?

Half the battle is gained if you never allow
yourself to say anything gloomy.

Lydia M. Child

Some doctors say that cheerful people resist
disease better than grumpy ones. The surly bird
catches the germ.

Nothing is more beautiful than cheerfulness
in an old face.

Jean Paul Richter

CHILDREN

Teach a child to choose the right path, and when
he is older he will remain upon it.

The Bible

The persons hardest to convince they're at the
retirement age are children at bedtime.

Shannon Fife

The thing that impresses me most about America is
the way parents obey their children.

Duke of Windsor

You can do anything with children if you only
play with them.

Prince Otto von Bismarck

There was never a child so lovely but his mother
was glad to get him asleep.

Emerson

No wonder kids are confused today. Half
of the adults tell them to find themselves;
the other half tell them to get lost.

Children are like mosquitoes—the moment they
stop making noises you know they're getting
into something.

Kids really brighten a household. They never turn off any lights.

Ralph Bus

Children are a real comfort in your old age—the problem is that they make you reach it sooner.

Oh, what a tangled web we weave when first we practice to conceive.

Don Herold

Kids used to ask where they came from, now they tell you where to go.

If any of us had a child that we thought was as bad as we know we are, we would have cause to start to worry.

Will Rogers

Children are natural mimics—they act like their parents in spite of every attempt to teach them good manners.

Children require guidance and sympathy far more than instruction.

Annie Sullivan

CHOICE

He who does not make a choice makes a choice.

CHRISTIAN

The Christian's chief occupational hazards are depression and discouragement.

John Stott

Too many Christians want to reach the Promised Land without going through the wilderness.

Whatever makes men good Christians makes them good citizens.

Daniel Webster

A man ought to live so that everybody knows he is a Christian . . . and most of all, his family ought to know.

D. L. Moody

CHRISTIANITY

Christianity has not been tried and found wanting; it has been found difficult and not tried.

G. K. Chesterton

He who shall introduce into public affairs the principles of primitive Christianity will change the face of the world.

Benjamin Franklin

CHRISTMAS

Shopping in crowded stores gives me Santa Claustrophobia.

For the millions who have been saving for a rainy day, Christmas is the monsoon season.

CHURCH

Division has done more to hide Christ from the view of men than all the infidelity that has ever been spoken.

George MacDonald

Where God has His church, the devil will have his chapel.

Though the church has many critics, it has no rivals.

CIRCUMSTANCES

People are always blaming their circumstances for what they are. I don't believe in circumstances. The people who get on in this world are the people who get up and look for the circumstances they want, and, if they can't find them, make them.

George Bernard Shaw

Circumstances are the rulers of the weak; they are but the instruments of the wise.

Samuel Lover

CLOTHES

Clothes make the man. Naked people have little or no influence in society.

Johnson

Freedom of the press means no-iron clothes.

COLLEGE

You can lead a boy to college but
you cannot make him think.

Elbert Hubbard

COMEDY

The whole object of comedy is to be yourself and the
closer you get to that, the funnier you will be.

Jerry Seinfeld

The only way to get a serious message across
is through comedy.

Woody Harrelson

Tragedy plus time equals comedy.

Steve Allen

COMFORT

The lust for comfort, that stealthy thing that enters
the house as a guest, and then becomes a host,
and then a master.

Most of the luxuries and many of the so-called
comforts of life are not only not indispensable, but
positive hindrances to the elevation of mankind.

Henry David Thoreau

We find comfort among those who agree with us—
growth among those who don't.

Frank A. Clark

COMMERCE

Our interest will be to throw open the doors of commerce, and to knock off all its shackles, giving perfect freedom to all persons for the vent of whatever they may choose to bring into our ports, and asking the same in theirs.

Thomas Jefferson

No nation was ever ruined by trade.

Benjamin Franklin

COMMITMENT

The ability to bind oneself emotionally and intellectually to an idea or task that needs to be completed.

COMMITTEE

You'll never find in no park or city, a monument to a committee.

Victoria Pasternak

Committee—a group of men who keep minutes and waste hours.

Milton Berle

The larger the number of people involved in any given decision, the greater the pressure for conformity.

I hate being placed on committees. They are always having meetings at which half are absent and the rest late.

Oliver Wendel I. Holmes, Jr.

COMMON MAN

It is a curious fact that when we get sick we want an uncommon doctor. If we have a construction job, we want an uncommon engineer. When we get into a war, we dreadfully want an uncommon admiral and an uncommon general. Only when we get into politics are we content with the common man.

Herbert Hoover

God must love the common man;
he made so many of them.

Abraham Lincoln

COMMON SENSE

Common sense is the knack of seeing things
as they are, and doing things as they
ought to be done.

Nothing astonishes men so much as common
sense and plain dealing.

Ralph Waldo Emerson

COMMUNICATION

Half of the world's problems are caused by poor communications. The other half are caused by good communications.

Never awake me when you have good news to announce, because with good news nothing presses; but when you have bad news, arouse me immediately, for then there is not an instant to be lost.

Napoleon Bonaparte

If you have anything to tell me of importance, for God's sake begin at the end.

Sara Jeanette Duncane

COMMUNISM

The theory of communism may be summed up in one sentence: Abolish all private property.

Karl Marx, Frieidrich Engels

Communism has nothing to do with love. Communism is an excellent hammer which we use to destroy our enemy.

Mao Tse-tung

Communism is a religion and only as we see it as a religion, though a secular religion, will we understand its power.

Elton Trueblood

COMPANION

I never found the companion that was so companionable as solitude.

Joseph Addison

Birds of a feather will gather together.

Robert Burton

Associate with men of good quality, if you esteem your own reputation; for it is better to be alone than in bad company.

George Washington

Tell me thy company and I will tell thee
what thou art.

Cervantes

COMPLAIN

When I complain, I do it because "it's good to get
things off my chest"; when you complain, I remind
you that "griping doesn't help anything."

Sydney Harris

I had no shoes and complained until I met a man
who had no feet.

Some people seem to go through life standing
at the complaint counter.

Fred Propp, Jr.

A constant dripping on a rainy day and a cranky
woman are much alike! You can no more stop her
complaints than you can stop the wind or hold onto
anything with oil-slick hands.

The Bible

COMPLIMENT

I can live for two months on a good compliment.

Mark Twain

Some people pay a compliment as if they
expected a receipt.

Frank Hubbard

When I did well, I heard it never;
When I did ill, I heard it ever.

COMPROMISE

If you just set out to be liked, you would be prepared to compromise on anything at any time, and you would achieve nothing.

Margaret Thatcher

Don't compromise yourself. You are all you've got.

He who goes with wolves learns to howl.

When one has peeled off the brown-paper wrapping of phrases and compromises, one finds—
just nothing at all.

Lytton Strachey

CONCEIT

There is one thing worse than a fool, and that is a man who is conceited.

The Bible

No man was ever so much deceived by another as by himself.

Greville

Conceit is a queer disease; it makes everybody sick but the one who has it.

Seest thou a man wise in his own conceit? There is more hope of a fool than of him.

The Bible

CONDUCT

I don't ever have any trouble in regulating my own conduct, but to keep other folks' straight is what bothers me.

Josh Billings

Let love be genuine; hate what is evil, hold fast to what is good; love one another with brotherly affection; outdo one another in showing honor. Never lag in zeal, be aglow with the Spirit, serve the Lord. Rejoice in your hope, be patient in tribulation, be constant in prayer.

The Bible

Twelve things to remember:
1. The value of time.
2. The success of perseverance.
3. The pleasure of working.
4. The dignity of simplicity.
5. The worth of character.
6. The power of kindness.
7. The influence of example.
8. The obligation of duty.
9. The wisdom of economy.
10. The virtue of patience.
11. The improvement of talent.
12. The joy of origination.

Marshall Field

CONFIDENCE

Never let the fear of striking out get in your way.

George Herman ("Babe") Ruth

If you once forfeit the confidence of your fellow citizens, you can never regain their respect and esteem.

Abraham Lincoln

CONFLICT

Face the conflict. To run from it will be
a continual race.

R. E. Phillips

Conflict can be an opportunity for growth or the tool
for destruction of relationships.

CONFORMITY

We forfeit three-fourths of ourselves in order to be like
other people.

Arthur Schopenhauer

CONGRESS

With Congress, every time they make a joke it's a law;
and every time they make a law it's a joke.

Will Rogers

Reader, suppose you were an idiot; and suppose you
were a member of Congress; but I repeat myself.

Mark Twain

A congressman had a nightmare—dreamed all
that money he was spending was his.

Transcendental meditation, by the way,
consists of sitting down, closing your eyes,
and letting your mind go blank. Congress has
been practicing it for years.

You don't have to join the navy to see the world.
You just become a congressman.

Senate office hours are from twelve to one with
an hour off for lunch.

Borge S. Kaufman

CONQUEROR

He is the greatest conqueror who has
conquered himself.

CONSCIENCE

A good conscience is a soft pillow.

I value people with a conscience.
It's like a beeper from God.

Robert Orben

There's no substitute for conscience. Unless, of
course, it's witnesses.

Franklin P. Jones

There is no better tranquilizer than a
clear conscience.

I am more afraid of my own heart than of the
pope and all his cardinals. I have within me
the great pope, self.

Martin Luther

Conscience: the inner voice which warns us that
someone may be looking.

H. L. Mencken

Labor to keep alive in your breast that little spark of celestial fire called conscience.

George Washington

CONSTITUTIONAL RIGHTS

Any time we deny any citizen the full exercise of his Constitutional rights, we are weakening our own claim to them.

Dwight D. Eisenhower

CONTEMPT

Perhaps the greatest sin one person can exert against another is contempt. To exercise contempt is to invite contempt. Any person who looks with contempt upon another sets in motion an evil force which rarely ever stops.

Charles Ashcraft

CONTENTMENT

After all, we didn't bring any money with us when we came into the world, and we can't carry away a single penny when we die. So we should be well satisfied without money if we have enough food and clothing.

The Bible

Contentment comes not so much from great wealth as from few wants.

Epictetus

The secret of contentment is knowing how to enjoy what you have, and to be able to lose all desire for things beyond your reach.

Lin Yutang

CONTROVERSY

When a thing ceases to be a subject of controversy, it ceases to be a subject of interest.

William Hazlitt

CONVERSATION

Think twice before you speak—and you'll find everyone talking about something else.

Francis Kitman

One of the reasons why so few people are to be found who seem sensible and pleasant in conversation is that almost everybody is thinking about what he wants to say himself, rather than about answering clearly what is being said to him. One secret of successful conversation is learning to disagree without being disagreeable. It isn't what but how you speak that makes all the difference. Ben Franklin used to remark diplomatically, "On this point, I agree. But on the other, if you don't mind, may I take exception?"

Jack Harrison Pollack

For good or ill, your conversation is your advertisement. Every time you open your mouth you let men look into your mind.

Bruce Barton

A single conversation with a wise man is better than ten years of study.

The value of the average conversation could be enormously improved by the constant use of four simple words: "I do not know."

Andre Maurois

CONVICTIONS

Beware lest we mistake our prejudices
for our convictions.

Harry A. Ironside

COOKBOOK

A practical cookbook is one that has a blank page
in the back—where you list the numbers of the
nearest delicatessen.

COOPERATION

You cannot sink someone else's end of the boat and
still keep your own afloat.

Charles Brower

COPYRIGHT

Copyright means copy it right out of the book.

CORRUPT

The more corrupt the state, the more
numerous the laws.

Tacitus

COUNSEL

Without wise leadership, a nation is in trouble; but
with good counselors there is safety.

The Bible

Plans go wrong with too few counselors; many counselors bring success.

The Bible

COURAGE

Far better it is to dare mighty things, to win glorious triumphs, even though checkered by failure, than to take rank with those poor spirits who neither enjoy much nor suffer much, because they live in the gray twilight that knows not victory or defeat.

Theodore Roosevelt

Courage is the mastery of fear, not the absence of fear.

Mark Twain

Courage is doing what you're afraid to do. There can be no courage unless you're scared.

Eddie Rickenbacker

Courage comes by being brave; fear comes by holding back.

Publilius Syrus

What would life be if we had no courage to attempt anything?

Vincent Van Gogh

It often takes more courage to change one's opinion than to stick to it.

George Christoph Lichtenberg

The test of tolerance comes when we are in a
majority; the test of courage comes when
we are in a minority.

Ralph W. Sockman

Courage takes many forms. There is physical
courage, there is moral courage. Then there is
a still higher type of courage—the courage
to brave pain, to live with it, to never let others
know of it, and to still find joy in life;
to wake up in the morning with an enthusiasm
for the day ahead.

Howard Cosell

This will remain the land of the free
only so long as it is the home of the brave.

Elmer Davis

COURT

Don't be hotheaded and rush to court! You may
start something you can't finish and go down before
your neighbor in shameful defeat. So discuss the
matter with him privately. Don't tell anyone else,
lest he accuse you of slander and you
can't withdraw what you said.

The Bible

COURTESY

Practice courtesy. You never know when it might
become popular again.

Bill Copeland

Nothing is more becoming in a great man than
courtesy and forbearance.

Cicero

Life is not so short but that there is always
time enough for courtesy.

Emerson

Never underestimate the power of simple courtesy.
Your courtesy may not be returned or
remembered, but discourtesy will.

Princess Jackson Smith

COURTING

He who would the daughter win, must
with the mother first begin.

If you would have a good wife, marry one
who has been a good daughter.

Thomas Fuller

COVET

Thou shalt not covet thy neighbor's house, thou shalt
not covet thy neighbor's wife, nor his manservant, nor
his maidservant, nor his ox, nor his ass, nor anything
that is thy neighbor's.

The Bible

The man who covets is always poor.

Claudian

CRAZY

One out of four people in this country is mentally imbalanced. Think of your three closest friends. If they seem okay, then you're the one.

Ann Landers

CREATIVITY

No matter how old you get, if you can keep the desire to be creative, you're keeping the man-child alive.

John Cassavetes

Creative minds always have been known to survive any kind of bad training.

Anna Freud

Creative minds are rarely tidy.

In my experience, the best creative work is never done when one is unhappy.

Albert Einstein

Creativity is so delicate a flower that praise tends to make it bloom, while discouragement often nips it in the bud. Any of us will put out more and better ideas if our efforts are truly appreciated.

Alexander Osborn

Creativity is essentially a lonely art. An even lonelier struggle. To some a blessing. To others a curse. It is in reality the ability to reach inside yourself and drag forth from your very soul an idea.

Lou Dorfsman

Teamwork may be good for morale, but when new ideas are needed, it's best to let people work on their own. Research shows that people who were left by themselves to think about subjects they considered relevant came up with three times as many ideas as those who brainstormed in groups. Researchers believe that when people work in groups, their creativity is inhibited by fear of criticism and real or perceived pressures to conform.

Creativity is inventing, experimenting, growing, taking risks, breaking rules, making mistakes, and having fun.

Mary Lou Cook

Our species is the only creative species, and it has only one creative instrument, the individual mind and spirit of a man. Nothing was ever created by two men. There are no good collaborations, whether in music, in art, in poetry, in mathematics, in philosophy. Once the miracle of creation has taken place, the group can build and extend it, but the group never invents anything. The preciousness lies in the lonely mind of a man.

John Steinbeck

CREDIBILITY

Do what is expected of you and you gain credibility. Don't do what is expected of you and you lose credibility.

CREDIT

The surest way to establish your credit is to work yourself into the position of not needing any.

Life was simpler before credit cards. You didn't
have to wait until the end of the month to
find out how poor you were.

CRIME

Most people fancy themselves innocent of those
crimes of which they cannot be convicted.

Seneca

The way to reduce crime is to convince the criminal
that, upon the commission of a crime, he will be
speedily apprehended, convicted, and punished.

Thomas A. Flannery

The only reason the crime rate was so low in rural
areas such as this was the close-knit social structure.
When everyone knows everyone else, crime was
either difficult or desperate.

John Fowles

Avoid carefully the first ill or mischief, for that
will breed a hundred more.

Keep thou from the opportunity and God will
keep thee from the sin.

Benjamin Franklin

Give a criminal enough rope and he'll tie
up a cashier.

I was going to read the report about
the rising crime rate . . . but
somebody stole it.

Will Rogers

CRISIS

The nearer any disease approaches to a crisis, the nearer it is to a cure. Danger and deliverance make their advances together; and it is only in the last push that one or the other takes the lead.

Thomas Paine

There cannot be a crisis next week. My schedule is already full.

Henry Kissinger

CRITIC

The writers against religion, whilst they oppose every system, are wisely careful never to set up any of their own.

Edmund Burke

A critic is a legless man who teaches running.

Channing Pollock

Pay no attention to what the critics say; there has never been set up a statue in honor of a critic.

Jean Sibelius

Those who have free seats at a play hiss first.

It is easier to pull down than to build up.

CRITICISM

It is a badge of honor to accept valid criticism.

The Bible

Criticism is a study by which men grow important
and formidable at very small expense.

Samuel Johnson

To escape criticism—do nothing,
say nothing, be nothing.

Elbert Hubbard

Criticism comes easier than craftsmanship.

Zeuxis

Tall trees catch much wind.

He has a right to criticize who has a heart to help.

Abraham Lincoln

Criticize by creating.

Michelangelo

If you get kicked from behind, it is because
you are out in front.

R. E. Phillips

Any fool can criticize, condemn and
complain—and most fools do.

Benjamin Franklin

Criticism is the art wherewith a critic tries to guess
himself into a share of the artist's fame.

George Jean Nathan

I find the pain of a little censure, even when
it is unfounded, is more acute than
the pleasure of much praise.

Thomas Jefferson

CURIOSITY

Life can be one dreary day after another or a Bagdad of fascinating things to keep learning. Get more out of every phase of your life—stay incurably curious.

L. Perry Wilbur

Curiosity is one of the permanent and certain characteristics of a vigorous intellect.

Samuel Johnson

DANGER

Wherever there is danger, there lurks opportunity;
whenever there is opportunity, there lurks danger.
The two are inseparable; they go together.

Earl Nightingale

The wise man in the storm prays to God, not for
safety from danger, but for deliverance from fear.

Emerson

Avoiding danger is no safer in the long run than
outright exposure. The fearful are caught as
often as the bold.

Helen Keller

Danger can never be overcome without danger.

DARE

Far better it is to dare mighty things, to win glorious
triumphs, even though checkered with defeat, than to

take rank with those poor spirits that neither enjoy much, nor suffer much, because they live in the gray twilight that knows not victory nor defeat.

Theodore Roosevelt

Why not go out on a limb? Isn't that where the fruit is?

Frank Scully

DEALS

Sometimes the best deals are the ones you don't make.

Bill Veeck

DEATH

Man weeps to think that he will die so soon; woman, that she was born so long ago.

H. L. Mencken

I'm not afraid to die. I just don't want to be there when it happens.

Woody Allen

I hate death; in fact I could live forever without it.

Pogo

My grandfather would look through the obituary columns and say to me, "Strange, isn't it, how everybody seems to die in alphabetical order."

Jackie Vernon

Death: to stop sinning suddenly.

Elbert Hubbard

DEBT

Pay all your debts except the debt of love
for others—never finish paying that!

The Bible

One can pay back the loan of gold, but one dies
forever in debt to those who are kind.

DECEPTION

Of all the agonies of life, that which is most
poignant and harrowing—that which for the time
annihilates reason and leaves our whole
organization one lacerated, mangled heart—is
the conviction that we have been deceived
where we placed all the trust of love.

Bulwer

You can fool some of the people all of the time, and
all of the people some of the time, but you cannot
fool all of the people all the time.

Abraham Lincoln

DECISION

Not to decide is to decide.

Harvey Cox

Decision is a sharp knife that cuts clean and straight;
indecision is a dull one that hacks and tears and
leaves ragged edges behind it.

Gordon Graham

When once a decision is reached and execution is the order of the day, dismiss absolutely all responsibility and care about the outcome.

Before you start looking for a peg, decide what hole you want to fill.

Once the facts are clear, the decisions jump out at you.

Peter Drucker

Take time to deliberate, but when the time for action has arrived, stop thinking and go in.

Napoleon Bonaparte

DEEDS

Good words without deeds are rushes and reeds.

Something attempted, something done.

Henry Wadsworth Longfellow

He has half the deed done, who has made a beginning.

Horace

DEFEAT

Oh, we all get run over—once in our lives. But one must pick oneself up again. And behave as if it were nothing.

Henrik Ibsen

How you handle defeat is not something to be taken lightly. You've got to think it through. Defeat is an art form. You've got to accept it, and you've got to go on. And once you do that, it's not bad.

Walter F. Mondale

The probability that we may fail in the struggle ought not to deter us from the support of a cause we believe to be just.

Abraham Lincoln

What is defeat? Nothing but education, nothing but the first step to something better.

Wendell Phillips

A defeat may be a victory in disguise.

DEFECTS

If we had no defects ourselves, we should not take so much pleasure in noting those of others.

Francois de La Rochefoucauld

DEMOCRACY

Democracy is based upon the conviction that there are extraordinary possibilities in ordinary people.

Harry Emerson Fosdick

The greatest blessing of our democracy is freedom. But in the last analysis, our only freedom is the freedom to discipline ourselves.

Bernard Baruch

What men value in the world is not rights,
but privileges.

H. L. Mencken

Democracy is the art and science of
running the circus from the monkey cage.

H. L. Mencken

Too many people expect wonders from democracy,
when the most wonderful thing of all is just having it.

Walter Winchell

Man's capacity for justice makes democracy
possible; but man's inclination to injustice
makes democracy necessary.

Democracy does not guarantee equality,
only equality of opportunity.

Irvin Kristol

The great thing about living in a democracy is that
you can say what you think without thinking.

Dwight D. Eisenhower

Two cheers for democracy: one because it
admits variety and two because
it permits criticism.

E. M. Forster

The death of democracy is not likely to be
an assassination from ambush. It will be a
slow extinction from apathy, indifference,
and undernourishment.

Robert M. Hutchins

Democracy is not a fragile flower:
still, it needs cultivating.

Ronald Reagan

The unhealthy gap between what we preach
in America and what we often practice creates a
moral dry rot that eats at the very foundation of
our democratic ideals and values.

Whitney Moore Young

When people start standing in line to get out of
this country instead of standing in line to get in,
then we can start worrying about our system.

Bernard Baruch

One of the most difficult decisions the individual
in a democracy faces is whether or not
he should forgo an immediate personal gain or
advantage for the good of his country.

Dwight D. Eisenhower

DEMOCRATS

If the Republicans will stop telling lies about
the Democrats, we will stop telling the
truth about them.

Adlai Stevenson

DEPENDABILITY

The bottom line of dependability is,
can you be trusted?

R. E. Phillips

A good horse never lacks a saddle.

DEPRESSION

One of the bad things about depression is that it drains us emotionally and makes us unable to handle things that normally would not get us down.
Billy Graham

Beware of allowing a tactless word, a rebuttal, a rejection to obliterate the whole sky.
Anais Nin

Noble deeds and hot baths are the best cures for depression.
Dodie Smith

DESIRE

Life contains but two tragedies. One is not to get your heart's desire; the other is to get it.
Socrates

A great law of human action—in order to make a man or a boy covet a thing, it is only necessary to make the thing difficult to attain.
Mark Twain

It is easier to suppress the first desire than to satisfy all that follow it.
Benjamin Franklin

DESPAIR

We should never despair; our situation before has been unpromising and has changed for the better, so I trust, it will again.
George Washington

Despair ruins some, presumption many.
Benjamin Franklin

DESPERATION

The mass of men lead lives of quiet desperation.
Henry David Thoreau

DETAILS

It is the little bits of things that fret and worry us; we
can dodge an elephant, but we can't a fly.
Josh Billings

DETERMINATION

Do what you can, with what you have,
where you are.
Theodore Roosevelt

Pray to God, but keep rowing to the shore.

If we all did the things we are capable of doing,
we would literally astound ourselves.
Thomas A. Edison

No farmer ever plowed a field
by turning it over in his mind.
George E. Woodbury

Determine that the thing can and shall be done,
and then we shall find the way.
Abraham Lincoln

No one would ever have crossed the ocean if he
could have gotten off the ship in the storm.

More men fail through lack of purpose
than lack of talent.

Billy Sunday

Never give in! Never give in! Never, never, never.
Never—in anything great or small, large or
petty—never give in except to convictions of
honor and good sense.

Winston Churchill

DEVIL

The devil can quote scripture for his purpose.

William Shakespeare

The devil is a better theologian than any
of us and is a devil still.

A. W. Tozer

DIAMOND

It is better to have old secondhand
diamonds than none at all.

Mark Twain

DICE

The best throw of the dice is to throw them away.

DIET

Blessed are those who hunger and thirst,
for they are sticking to their diets.

Troy Gordon

There's a new diet that is supposed to really work. You only get to eat when there's good news.

When it comes to eating, you can sometimes help yourself more by helping yourself less.

Richard Armour

DIFFERENCES

We all live under the same sky, but we don't all have the same horizon.

Konrad Adenauer

DIFFICULTIES

Difficulty, my brethren, is the nurse of greatness—a harsh nurse, who roughly rocks her foster-children into strength and athletic proportion.

Undertake something that is difficult; it will do you good. Unless you try to do something beyond what you have already mastered, you will never grow.

Ronald E. Osborn

Many men owe the grandeur of their lives to their tremendous difficulties.

Charles H. Spurgeon

There are two ways of meeting difficulties: You alter the difficulties or you alter yourself to meet them.

Phyllis Bottome

The best way out of a difficulty is through it.

DILIGENCE

One worthwhile task carried to a successful conclusion is worth half-a-hundred half-finished tasks.
B. C. Forbes

DIPLOMACY

A diplomat is a man who remembers a woman's
birthday and forgets her age.

The principle of give and take is the principle of
diplomacy—give one and take ten.
Mark Twain

Diplomacy: The business of handling a porcupine
without disturbing the quills.

The best way to knock the chip off your neighbor's
shoulder is to pat him on the back.

DIRECTION

Any time the going seems easier, better check and
see if you're not going downhill.

The world stands aside to let anyone pass who
knows where he is going.
David Staff Jordan

DISAPPOINTMENT

Blessed be he who expects nothing, for he shall
never be disappointed.
Jonathan Swift

DISCERNMENT

Any story sounds true until someone tells the other side and sets the record straight.

The Bible

Judge not of actions by their mere effect;
Dive to the center and the cause detect;
Great deeds from meanest springs
may take their course,
And smallest virtues from
a mighty source.

Alexander Pope

DISCIPLINE

If you refuse to discipline your son, it proves you don't love him; for if you love him you will be prompt to punish him.

The Bible

Sometimes mere words are not enough—discipline is needed. For the words may not be heeded.

The Bible

He who will not answer to the rudder must answer to the rocks.

DISCOURAGEMENT

Never tell a young person that something cannot be done. God may have been waiting for countless centuries for somebody ignorant enough of the impossibility to do that thing.

I never allow myself to become discouraged under any circumstances. . . .The three great essentials to achieve anything worthwhile are, first, hard work; second, stick-to-itiveness; third, common sense.

Thomas A. Edison

DISCRETION

A wise man restrains his anger and overlooks insults. This is to his credit.

The Bible

If thou art a master, be sometimes blind, if a servant, sometimes deaf.

Thomas Fuller

DISHONEST

To speak ill of others is a dishonest way of praising ourselves.

Ariel and Will Durant

DISTRUST

To distrust is to be lonely.

R. E. Phillips

DIVERSITY

Keep out of ruts; a rut is something which if traveled in too much, becomes a ditch.

Arthur Guiterman

DOCTOR

The best doctors in the world are Dr. Diet,
Dr. Quiet, and Dr. Merryman.

Jonathan Swift

Our doctor would never really operate unless it was
necessary. He was just that way. If he didn't need
the money, he wouldn't lay a hand on you.

Herb Shriner

The doctor is to be feared more than the disease.

Whenever a doctor cannot do good, he
must be kept from doing harm.

Hippocrates

A doctor is a man who writes prescriptions till the
patient either dies or is cured by nature.

John Taylor

A doctor's reputation is made by the number
of eminent men who die under his care.

George Bernard Shaw

A good laugh and a long sleep are the best
cures in the doctor's book.

DOUBT

Don't doubt in the dark what God has
revealed in the light.

V. Raymond Edman

I respect faith, but doubt is what gets
you an education.
Wilson Mizner

When in doubt who will win, be neutral.

DREAMS

Dreams are great. When they disappear you
may still be here, but you will have ceased to live.
Lady Nancy Astor

If you want your dreams to come true, don't sleep.
If dreams all came true, one would fear to fall asleep.

DRINKING

Wine gives false courage; hard liquor leads to brawls;
what fools men are to let it master them, making
them reel drunkenly down the street!
The Bible

One reason I don't drink is that I want to know
when I am having a good time.

DRIVE-IN BANKING

Drive-in banking was invented so cars could go in
and see their real owners.

DUTIES

When you have a number of disagreeable duties to
perform, always do the most disagreeable first.
Josiah Quincy

Knowledge of your duties is the most essential part of the philosophy of life. If you avoid duty, you avoid action. The world demands results.

George W. Goethals

Make it a point to do something every day that you don't want to do. This is the golden rule for acquiring the habit of doing your duty without pain.

Mark Twain

Our main business is not to see what lies dimly at a distance, but to do what lies clearly at hand.

Thomas Carlyle

I believe that every right implies a responsibility;
every opportunity, an obligation;
every possession, duty.

John D. Rockefeller, Jr.

I long to accomplish a great and noble task, but it is my chief duty to accomplish small tasks as if they were great and noble.

Helen Keller

What better fate for a man than to die in the performance of his duty?

Douglas MacArthur

EARNESTNESS

Earnestness is the salt of eloquence.
Victor Hugo

Earnestness is enthusiasm tempered by reason.
Blaise Pascal

ECONOMICS

You cannot strengthen the weak by weakening the strong. You cannot help the wage-earner by pulling down the wage-payer. You cannot help the poor by destroying the rich. You cannot help men permanently by doing for them what they could and should do for themselves.
Abraham Lincoln

ECONOMY

In layman's terms, a recession is when you have to tighten your belt and a depression is when you have no belt to tighten. When you have no pants to hold up, that's called a panic.

An economist is an expert who will know tomorrow why the things he predicted yesterday didn't happen today.

Henry Ford

Prosperity is something that businessmen create for politicians to take the credit for.

Economists are people who see something work in practice and wonder if it would work in theory.

Ronald Reagan

EDITOR

Editor: a person employed on a newspaper, whose business it is to separate the wheat from the chaff, and to see that the chaff is printed.

Elbert Hubbard

An editor is a man who knows what he wants, but doesn't know what it is.

Walter Davenport

EDUCATION

Education is what's left over when you subtract what you've forgotten from what you've learned.

Sixty years ago I knew everything; now I know nothing; education is a progressive discovery of our own ignorance.

Will Durant

Perhaps the most valuable result of all
education is the ability to make yourself
do the thing you have to do, when it ought
to be done, whether you like it or not.

Thomas Huxley

Education is hanging around until you've caught on.

Robert Frost

The purpose of education is to provide
everyone with the opportunity to learn how best he
may serve the world.

If a man empties his purse into his head,
no one can take it from him.

Benjamin Franklin

If nobody dropped out at the eighth grade, who
would hire the college graduates?

Economists report that a college education
adds many thousands of dollars to a man's
lifetime income—which he then spends
sending his son to college.

Bill Vaughan

EFFORT

If you don't scale the mountain, you can't
see the view.

Do a little more each day than
you think you possibly can.

Lowell Thomas

I have found it advisable not to give too much heed
to what people say when I am trying to accomplish

something of consequence. Invariably they proclaim it can't be done. I deem that the very best time to make the effort.

Calvin Coolidge

EGGS

Put all your eggs in one basket, and—watch that basket.

Mark Twain

EGO

The last time I saw him he was walking down Lover's Lane holding his own hand.

Fred Allen

An egotist is not a man who thinks too much of himself. He is a man who thinks too little of other people.

J. F. Newton

ELDERLY

People who don't cherish their elderly have forgotten whence they came and whither they go.

Ramsey Clark

ELOQUENCE

The finest eloquence is that which gets things done.

David Lloyd George

ENCOURAGEMENT

Appreciation is thanking, recognition is seeing, and encouragement is bringing hope for the future.

Anxious hearts are very heavy but a word of encouragement does wonders!

The Bible

Correction does much, but encouragement does more. Encouragement after censure is as the sun after a shower.

Johann Wolfgang von Goethe

ENDURANCE

Endure and persist; this pain will turn to your good.

Ovid

And let us not get tired of doing what is right, for after a while we will reap a harvest of blessing if we don't get discouraged and give up.

The Bible

ENEMIES

Could we read the sacred history of our enemies, we should find in each man's life, sorrow and suffering enough to disarm all hostility.

Henry Wadsworth Longfellow

The Bible tells us to love our neighbors, and also to love our enemies; probably because they are generally the same people.

G. K. Chesterton

Do not rejoice when your enemy meets trouble. Let there be no gladness when he falls—for the Lord may be displeased with you and stop punishing him!

The Bible

If your enemy is hungry, give him food! If he is thirsty, give him something to drink! This will make him feel ashamed of himself, and God will reward you.

The Bible

The best way to destroy your enemy is to make him your friend.

Abraham Lincoln

If you want to make enemies, try to change something.

Woodrow Wilson

ENTHUSIASM

Both enthusiasm and pessimism are contagious. Which one do you spread?

If you aren't fired with enthusiasm, you will be fired with enthusiasm.

Vince Lombardi

When a man dies, if he can pass enthusiasm along to his children, he has left them an estate of incalculable value.

Thomas A. Edison

Every production of genius must be the production of enthusiasm.

Benjamin Disraeli

Nothing is so contagious as enthusiasm;
it moves stones, it charms brutes. Enthusiasm
is the genius of sincerity and thus accomplishes no
victories without it.

Bulwer-Lytton

I studied the lives of great men and famous women,
and I found that the men and women who got
to the top were those who did the jobs
they had in hand, with everything they had
of energy and enthusiasm and hard work.

Harry S. Truman

ENVY

If there is any sin more deadly than envy,
it is being pleased at being envied.

Richard Armour

Envy takes the joy, happiness, and
contentment out of living.

Billy Graham

As a moth gnaws a garment, so doth
envy consume a man.

St. Chrysostom

EQUALITY

We are all alike, on the inside.

Mark Twain

Inferiors revolt in order that they may be equal, and
equals that they may be superior.

Aristotle

ERROR

An error gracefully acknowledged is a victory won.
Caroline L. Gascoigne

An error is more dangerous in proportion to the degree of truth it contains.
Henri Frederic Amiel

Error is the discipline through which we advance.
William Ellery Channing

ETHICS

I would rather be the man who bought the Brooklyn Bridge than the man who sold it.
Will Rogers

EVENTS

When I can't handle events, I let them handle themselves.
Henry Ford

Events of great consequence often spring from trifling circumstances.
Livy

If men could regard the events of their own lives with more open minds, they would frequently discover that they did not really desire the things they failed to obtain.
Andre Maurois

EVIL

Repay evil with good and you deprive the
evildoer of all the pleasure of his wickedness.

Leo Tolstoy

Of two evils, choose neither.

Charles H. Spurgeon

Woe unto them that call evil good, and good evil.

The Bible

When good people in any country cease their
vigilance and struggle, then evil men prevail.

Pearl S. Buck

EVOLUTION

The evolutionists seem to know everything about the
missing link except the fact that it is missing.

G. K. Chesterton

There is no more reason to believe that man
descended from some inferior animal than
there is to believe that a stately mansion has
descended from a small cottage.

W. J. Bryan

Once I was a tadpole when I began to begin.
Then I was a frog with my tail tucked in.
Next I was a monkey on a coconut tree.
Now I am a doctor with a Ph.D.

EXAGGERATION

There are people so addicted to exaggeration that
they can't tell the truth without lying.

Josh Billings

EXAMPLE

Example is not the main thing in influencing others.
It is the only thing.

Albert Schweitzer

Few things are harder to put up with than the
annoyance of a good example.

Mark Twain

The first great gift we can bestow on others
is a good example.

Thomas Morell

EXCELLENCE

The pursuit of excellence is gratifying and healthy.
The pursuit of perfection is frustrating, neurotic,
and a terrible waste of time.

Edwin Bliss

The secret of joy is contained in
one word—excellence. To know how to do
something well is to enjoy it.

Pearl S. Buck

EXCUSE

Win without boasting. Lose without excuse.
Albert Payson Terhune

The list below is the current popularity rating for excuses. To save time for me and for yourself, please give your excuse by number.

1. I thought I told you.
2. That's the way we've always done it.
3. No one told me to go ahead.
4. I didn't think it was very important.
5. I'm so busy I just can't get around to it.
6. Why bother? The admiral won't buy it.
7. I didn't know you were in a hurry for it.
8. That's his job, not mine.
9. I forgot.
10. I'm waiting for an OK.
11 That's not in my department.
12. How did I know this was different?
13. Wait 'til the boss comes back and ask him.

EXERCISE

The only exercise some people get is jumping to conclusions, running down their friends, sidestepping responsibility, dodging issues, passing the buck, and pushing their luck.

Whenever I feel like exercise, I lie down until the feeling passes.
Maynard Robert Hutchins

The person who does not find time for exercise may have to find time for illness.

EXPECTATION

Do not anticipate trouble, or worry about
what may never happen.
Keep in the sunlight.
Benjamin Franklin

EXPECTATIONS

The more reasonable we are in our expectations,
the fewer disappointments we will have in life.
A. Nielen

EXPENSE

If your outgo exceeds your income, your
upkeep will be your downfall.
John Poure

The cost of living is going up and the chance
of living is going down.
Flip Wilson

EXPERIENCE

The best substitute for experience is being sixteen.
Raymond Duncan

Truth divorced from experience will always dwell
in the realms of doubt.
Henry Krause

I have but one lamp by which my feet
are guided, and that is the lamp of experience.
Patrick Henry

EXPERT

An expert is one who knows more and
more about less and less.

Nicholas Murray Butler

An expert is a man who makes his mistakes quietly.

Make three correct guesses consecutively and you
will establish a reputation as an expert.

Laurence J. Peter

EYESIGHT

There is no lovelier way to thank God for
your sight than by giving a helping hand to
someone in the dark.

Helen Keller

FACES

Silence will not betray your thoughts but
the expression on your face will.
Humor has a hundred faces; tragedy only a few.
H. G. Mendelson

FACTS

Get your facts first, and then you can distort them
as much as you please.
Mark Twain

Facts are stubborn things.
Smollett

FAILURE

The men who try to do something and fail are
infinitely better than those who try to do
nothing and succeed.
Lloyd Jones

Ninety percent of all failures result from people quitting too soon.

I don't know the key to success, but the key to failure is trying to please everybody.
Bill Cosby

Whenever you fall, pick something up.
Oswald Avery

Failure is a far better teacher than success, but she hardly ever finds any apples on her desk.

FAIRNESS

Years have taught me at least one thing and that is not to try to avoid an unpleasant fact, but rather to grasp it firmly and let the other person observe I am at least treating him fairly. Then he, it has been my observation, will treat me in the same spirit.
Benjamin Franklin

How seldom we weigh our neighbor in the same balance with ourselves.
Thomas à Kempis

FAITH

If we desire an increase of faith, we must consent to its testings.

We live by faith or we do not live at all. Either we venture—or we vegetate. If we venture, we do so by faith simply because we cannot know the end of anything at its beginning. We risk marriage on faith or we stay single. We prepare for a profession

by faith or we give up before we start. By faith we
move mountains of opposition or we are
stopped by molehills.

Harold Walker

Faith is the substance of things hoped for,
the evidence of things not seen.

The Bible

Fight the good fight of faith.

The Bible

FAITHFULNESS

Nothing in life can take the place of faithfulness
and dependability. It is one of the greatest virtues.
Brilliance, genius, competence—all are subservient
to the quality of faithfulness.

Walace Fridy

A faithful employee is as refreshing as a cool day
in the hot summertime.

The Bible

Show me a man who cannot bother to do little
things and I'll show you a man who cannot be
trusted to do big things.

Lawrence D. Bell

FAME

Fame is a fickle food upon a shifting plate.

Emily Dickinson

Fame is proof that the people are gullible.

Emerson

I would rather that men ask . . . why I have no
statue than why I have one.

Cato the Elder

FAMILIARITY

Familiarity breeds contempt.

Publilius Syrus

Familiarity breeds contempt—and children.

Mark Twain

Though familiarity may not breed contempt, it takes
off the edge of admiration.

William Hazlitt

FAMILY

Happy families are all alike; every unhappy
family is unhappy in its own way.

Leo Tolstoy

A modern home is where the TV set is
better adjusted than the kids.

No family should attempt an auto trip if the kids
outnumber the car windows.

Terresa Bloomingdale

A family is a unit composed not only of
children but of men, women, an occasional
animal, and the common cold.

Ogden Nash

No matter how many communes anybody invents,
the family always creeps back.

Margaret Mead

It is my conviction that the family is God's basic unit
in society. God's most important unit in society. No
wonder then . . . we are in a holy war for the survival
of the family. Before a nation collapses the families
of that nation must go down first. What is a local
church? Nothing but a congregation of families.

Jerry Falwell

FASHION

I see that fashion wears out more apparel
than the man.

William Shakespeare

Fashion is a form of ugliness so intolerable that we
have to alter it every six months.

Oscar Wilde

FATHER

It is a wonderful heritage to have an honest father.

The Bible

One father is more than a hundred schoolmasters.

George Herbert

He can climb the highest mountain or swim the
biggest ocean. He can fly the fastest plane and fight
the strongest tiger. But most of the time he just
carries out the garbage.

The most important thing a father can
do for his children is to love
their mother.

Theodore Hesburgh

It doesn't matter who my father was; it matters
who I remember he was.

Anne Sexton

FATIGUE

Fatigue is the best pillow.

Benjamin Franklin

Nothing is so fatiguing as the eternal hanging
on of an uncompleted task.

William James

FAULTS

Deal with the faults of others as gently
as with your own.

Every man should have a fair-sized cemetery in
which to bury the faults of his friends.

Henry Ward Beecher

The greatest of all faults is to be conscious of none.

Thomas Carlyle

Faults are thick where love is thin.

James Howell

FEAR

To live with fear and not be afraid is the final
test of maturity.

Edward Weeks

Nothing in life is to be feared. It is only
to be understood.

Marie Curie

The only thing we have to fear is fear itself.

Franklin D. Roosevelt

He who fears he will suffer, already suffers
because of his fear.

Michel de Montaigne

The fear of the Lord is the beginning of knowledge.

The Bible

Keep your fears to yourself, but share
your courage with others.

Robert Louis Stevenson

FEELINGS

The man who is always having his feelings
hurt is about as pleasing a companion
as a pebble in a shoe.

Elbert Hubbard

Never apologize for showing feelings. Remember
that when you do, you apologize for the truth.

Benjamin Disraeli

It is terribly amusing how many different climates of feeling one can go through in one day.

Anne Morrow Lindbergh

FIGHT

The time to win a fight is before it starts.

Frederick W. Lewis

FISHING

There is no use in walking five miles to fish when you can depend on being as unsuccessful near home.

God does not deduct from man's allotted time those hours spent in fishing.

Do not tell fish stories where the people know you; but particularly, don't tell them where they know the fish.

FLAG

The cross, the flag are the embodiment of our ideals and teach us not only how to live but how to die.

Douglas MacArthur

FLASHLIGHT

A flashlight is what you carry dead batteries in.

FLATTERY

Flattery is a trap; evil men are caught in it, but good men stay away and sing for joy.

The Bible

When flatterers meet, the devil goes to dinner.

Defoe

Nothing is so great an instance of ill manners as flattery. If you flatter all the company you please none; if you flatter only one or two, you affront all the rest.

Jonathan Swift

A man that flattereth his neighbor spreadeth a net for his feet.

The Bible

FLIRTING

Flirting is wishful winking.

FOCUS

What we steadily, consciously, habitually think we are, that we tend to become.

John Cowper Powers

I recommend you take care of the minutes, for the hours will take care of themselves.

Lord of Chesterfield

He had so many irons in the fire that he was never able to forge any single one into a weapon with which to conquer his world.

Curtis Dahl

One never notices what has been done; one can only see what remains to be done.

Marie Curie

FOOD

I am allergic to food. Every time I eat,
it breaks out in fat.

Jennifer Greene Duncan

The most dangerous food a man can eat is wedding cake.

As a child my family's menu consisted of two choices: take it, or leave it.

Buddy Hackett

FOOL

A fool thinks he needs no advice, but a wise man listens to others.

The Bible

Expectation is the fool's income.
Let us be thankful for the fools. But for them the rest of us could not succeed.

Mark Twain

A man never knows what a fool he is until he hears himself imitated by one.

Herbert Tree

April 1 is the day upon which we are reminded of what we are on the other 364.

Mark Twain

The fool hath said in his heart, "There is no God."

The Bible

FOOTBALL

If a man watches three football games in a row, he should be declared legally dead.

Erma Bombeck

FORBEARANCE

Cultivate forbearance till your heart yields a fine crop of it. Pray for a short memory as to all unkindnesses.

Charles H. Spurgeon

FORBIDDEN

The more things are forbidden, the more popular they become.

FORBIDDEN FRUIT

Forbidden fruit is responsible for many a bad jam.

FORCE

Justice without force is powerless; force without justice is tyrannical.

Blaise Pascal

A man convinced against his will
is of the same opinion still.

Samuel Butler

FOREIGN AID

Too often foreign aid is when the poor people of a
rich nation send their money to the rich people
of a poor nation.

FORESIGHT

It's helpful to look at your life and ask: "If I had
one more year to live, what would I do?"
We all have things we want to achieve.
Don't just put them off—do them now!

John Goddard

FORGETFULNESS

More important than learning how to recall
things is finding ways to forget things that are
cluttering the mind.

Eric Butterworth

There are three things I always forget. Names,
faces—the third I can't remember.

Italo Suevo

I've a grand memory for forgetting.

Robert Louis Stevenson

FORGIVENESS

It is very easy to forgive others their mistakes;
it takes more grit and gumption to forgive them
for having witnessed your own.
Always forgive your enemies—nothing
annoys them so much.

Oscar Wilde

He that cannot forgive others breaks the
bridge over which he must pass himself; for every
man has need to be forgiven.

Thomas Fuller

Forgiveness is the fragrance the violet
sheds on the heel that has crushed it.

Mark Twain

There's no point in burying a hatchet if you're
going to put up a marker on the site.

Sydney Harris

A good memory is fine—but the ability to forget
is the true test of greatness.

Forgiveness is not a feeling but a promise
or commitment to three things:
1. I will not use it against them in the future,
2. I will not talk to others about them,
3. I will not dwell on it myself.

Jay E. Adams

A Christian will find it cheaper to pardon than to
resent. Forgiveness saves the expense of anger,
the cost of hatred, the waste of spirits.

Hannah More

FORTUNE

Fortune favors the bold but abandons the timid.

FRANKNESS

Frankness invites frankness.
Emerson

It is an honor to receive a frank reply.
The Bible

FREEDOM

Freedom is like a coin. It has the word *privilege* on one side and *responsibility* on the other. It does not have privilege on both sides. There are too many today who want everything involved in privilege but refuse to accept anything that approaches the sense of responsibility.
Joseph Sizoo

Personal liberty is the paramount essential to human dignity and human happiness.
Bulwer Lytton

Since the general civilizations of mankind I believe there are more instances of the abridgment of the freedom of the people by gradual and silent encroachments of those in power than by violent and sudden usurpations.
James Madison

The condition upon which God has given liberty to man is eternal vigilance.
John Philpot Curran

Who has lost his freedom has nothing else to lose.

The cost of freedom is always high, but Americans
have always paid it. And one path we shall
never choose, and that is the path of
surrender, or submission.

John F. Kennedy

When the freedom they wished for most was
freedom from responsibility, then Athens ceased
to be free and was never free again.

Edith Hamilton

To enjoy freedom we have to control ourselves.

Those who deny freedom to others deserve it
not for themselves, and, under a just God,
cannot long retain it.

Abraham Lincoln

Is life so dear, or peace so sweet, as to be purchased
at the price of chains and slavery? Forbid it, Almighty
God! I know not what course others may take; but as
for me, give me liberty, or give me death!

Patrick Henry

The sound of tireless voices is the price
we pay for the right to hear the music
of our own opinions.

Adlai Stevenson

Freedom does not mean the right to do whatever
we please, but rather to do whatever we ought. . . .
The right to do whatever we please reduces
freedom to a physical power and forgets that
freedom is a moral power.

Fulton J. Sheen

Freedom of speech does not give a person
the right to shout "Fire!" in a crowded theater.

Oliver Wendell Holmes

I would rather be exposed to the inconveniences
attending too much liberty than those attending too
small a degree of it.

Thomas Jefferson

FRIEND

Nothing is there more friendly to a man than
a friend in need.

Plautus

Friend: One who knows all about you
and loves you just the same.

Before borrowing money from a friend
decide which you need most.

Never speak ill of yourself. Your friends will always
say enough on that subject.

Charles Maurice de Talleyrand

Friendship may, and often does, grow into love; but
love never subsides into friendship.

Lord Byron

Real friends are those who, when you've
made a fool of yourself, don't feel that you've
done a permanent job.

I desire so to conduct the affairs of this administration
that if at the end, when I come to lay down

the reins of power, I have lost every other friend
on earth, I shall at least have one friend left,
and that friend shall be down inside of me.

Abraham Lincoln

Friends are made by many acts—and
lost by only one.

A friend is one who comes to you
when all others leave.

Good company in a journey makes
the way seem the shorter.

Izaak Walton

One should keep his friendships in constant repair.

Samuel Johnson

My best friend is the one who brings
out the best in me.

Henry Ford

He who seeks friends without faults stays
forever without friends.

A friend is a person who goes around saying nice
things about you behind your back.

The only way to have a friend is to be one.

Emerson

Animals are such agreeable friends—they ask no
questions, they pass no criticisms.

George Eliot

I had only one friend, my dog. My wife was mad at me, and I told her a man ought to have at least two friends. She agreed—and bought me another dog.

Pepper Rodgers

FRUSTRATION

Frustration is the emotional battle we face when tasks or goals are not accomplished.

FUNERAL

The reason so many people showed up at his funeral was because they wanted to make sure he was dead.

Samuel Goldwyn

FUNNY

Everything is funny as long as it is happening to somebody else.

Will Rogers

FUTURE

The best thing about the future is that it comes only one day at a time.

Abraham Lincoln

My interest is in the future because I am going to spend the rest of my life there.

Charles F. Kettering

The best business you can go into you will find in your father's farm or in his workshop. If you have no family or friends to aid you, and no prospect open to you there, turn your face to the great West, and there build up a home and fortune.

Horace Greeley

GAMBLE

He who gambles picks his own pocket.

The only man that makes money following the races
is the one who does so with a broom and shovel.
Elbert Hubbard

Gambling: The sure way of getting
nothing for something.
Wilson Mizner

GARDEN

One of the most delightful things about a garden is
the anticipation it provides.
W. E. Johns

GENERATION

I was born in the wrong generation.
When I was a young man, no one had

any respect for youth. Now I am an old
man and no one has any respect for age.

Bertrand Russell

GENEROUS

We're all generous, but with different things, like
time, money, talent—criticism.

Frank A. Clark

GENIUS

Men give me credit for genius; but all the genius
I have lies in this: When I have a subject on hand
I study it profoundly.

Alexander Hamilton

GENTLEMAN

To be born a gentleman is an accident—to die
one is an accomplishment.

A gentleman is a gentleman the world over;
loafers differ.

George Bernard Shaw

GENTLENESS

Nothing is so strong as gentleness;
nothing so gentle as real strength.

St. Francis de Sales

Gentleness springs from great strength.

R. E. Phillips

GIFTS

We should give as we would receive, cheerfully,
quickly, and without hesitation; for there is no grace
in a benefit that sticks to the fingers.

Seneca

If you have much, give of your wealth;
if you have little, give of your heart.

GIVING

It's better to give than to lend, and it costs
about the same.

Philip Gibbs

If you are not generous with a meager income,
you will never be generous with abundance.

Harold Nye

When it comes to giving, some people
stop at nothing.

No person was ever honored for what he received.
Honor has been the reward for what he gave.

Calvin Coolidge

You only keep what you give away.

R. E. Phillips

It is one of the most beautiful compensations of
this life that no man can sincerely try to help
another without helping himself.

Emerson

Do your giving while you're living, so you're knowing where it's going.
Donald Sumner French

GLORY

Glory to God in the highest, and on earth peace, good will toward men.
The Bible

GLUTTONY

Gluttony is an emotional escape, a sign something is eating us.
Peter De Vries

GOAL

The self which desires a thing is not the self which at last possesses that thing. As one approaches any goal, it seems more and more reasonable that one should reach it, and desire commences to look beyond.
Richard P. Wilbur

Do not turn back when you are just at the goal.
Publilius Syrus

GOD

What a vast distance there is between knowing God and loving Him!
Blaise Pascal

A pastor visited a family whose son had been killed in an automobile accident. He heard the mother rail out at him: "Where was your God when my boy was killed?" He quietly said, "The same place He was when His Son was killed."

Roger Lovette

You have laughed God out of your schools, out of your books, and out of your life, but you cannot laugh Him out of your death.

Dagobert Runes

A true love to God must begin with a delight in His holiness, and not with a delight in any other attribute; for no other attribute is truly lovely without this.

Jonathan Edwards

Let us weigh the gain and the loss in wagering that God is, but let us consider the two possibilities. If you gain, you gain all; if you lose you lose nothing. Hesitate not, then, to wager that He is.

Blaise Pascal

When God would educate a man He compels him to learn bitter lessons. He sends him to school to the necessities rather than to the graces, that, by knowing all suffering, he may know also the eternal consolation.

Celia Burleigh

Live with men as if God saw you, and talk to God as if men were listening.

Athenodorus

God moves in a mysterious way
His wonders to perform;
He plants His footsteps in the sea
And rides upon the storm.

William Cowper

I can see how a man can look down upon the
earth and be an atheist, but I cannot conceive
how he could look up into the heavens
and say there is no God.

Abraham Lincoln

Often God has to shut a door in our face, so
that He can subsequently open the door through
which He wants us to go.

Catherine Marshall

GOLF

Golf is like a love affair: If you don't take it
seriously, it's no fun; If you do take it seriously,
it breaks your heart.

Arnold Daly

Golf is a good walk spoiled.

GOOD DEEDS

The smallest good deed is better than the
grandest intention.

GOOD HUMOR

Good humor makes all things tolerable.

Henry Ward Beecher

Do not take life too seriously. You will never
get out of it alive.

Elbert Hubbard

GOOD NAME

A good name, like good will, is got by many
actions and lost by one.

Lord Jeffrey

GOOD WORKS

He rightly reads Scripture who turns
words into deeds.

Saint Bernard of Clairvaux

GOSPEL

There are two things to do about the gospel:
believe it and behave it.

Susannah Wesley

GOSSIP

An evil man sows strife; gossip separates
the best of friends.

The Bible

Don't tell your secrets to a gossip unless you want
them broadcast to the world.

The Bible

I am more deadly than the screaming shell from the
howitzer. I win without killing. I tear down homes,
break hearts, and wreck lives. I travel on the wings
of the wind. No innocence is strong enough to
intimidate me, no purity pure enough to daunt me. I
have no regard for truth, no respect for justice, no

mercy for the defenseless. My victims are as numerous as the sands of the sea, and often as innocent. I never forget and seldom forgive. My name is Gossip.

Morgan Blake

He who relates the faults of others to you will relate your faults to the other fellow.

Not everyone repeats gossip. Some improve it.

Franklin P. Jones

Conversation between Adam and Eve must have been difficult at times because they had nobody to talk about.

Agnes Repplier

Hear no evil, see no evil, speak no evil—and you'll never be invited to a party.

What you don't see with your eyes, don't invent with your mouth.

GOVERNMENT

A house divided against itself cannot stand—I believe this government cannot endure permanently half-slave and half-free.

Abraham Lincoln

The impersonal hand of government can never replace the helping hand of a neighbor.

Hubert Humphrey

Govern yourself and you can govern
the world.

The whole of government consists in
the art of being honest.

Thomas Jefferson

It's a good thing we don't get all the
government we pay for.

Nothing is easier than the expenditure of public
money. It doesn't appear to belong to anyone.
The temptation is overwhelming to bestow
it on somebody.

Calvin Coolidge

There's no trick to being a humorist when you have
the whole government working for you.

Will Rogers

My experience in government is that when things are
non-controversial, beautifully coordinated, and all the
rest, it must be that there is not much going on.

John F. Kennedy

Why has the government been instituted at all?
Because the passions of men will not conform to the
dictates of reason and justice, without constraint.

Alexander Hamilton

My reading of history convinces me that most bad
government has grown out of too much government.

John Sharp Williams

Everyone wants to live at the expense of
the state. They forget that the state lives at the
expense of everyone.

Frederic Bastiat

Too bad that all the people who know how to run the
country are busy driving taxicabs and cutting hair.

George Burns

The single most exciting thing you encounter in
government is competence, because it is so rare.

Daniel Patrick Moynihan

The ten most terrifying words in the English
language are "I'm from the government and I'm
here to help you."

The best minds are not in government. If any
were, business would hire them away.

Ronald Reagan

Trying to make things work in government is
sometimes like trying to sew a button
on a custard pie.

Admiral Hyman G. Rickover

One of the greatest delusions in the world is
the hope that the evils in this world are to be
cured by legislation.

Thomas B. Reed

When you think of the government debt
the next generation must pay off, it's no wonder
the baby yells when it's born.

I have always stated that the nearest
thing to eternal life we'll ever

see on the earth is a
government program.
Ronald Reagan

The government is my shepherd I need not work. It
alloweth me to lie down on a good job, it leadeth me
beside still factories; it destroyeth my initiative. It
leadeth me in the path of a parasite for politics' sake.
Yea, though I walk through the valley of laziness and
deficit spending, I will feel no evil, for the government
is with me. It prepareth an economic Utopia for me
by appropriating the earnings of my grandchildren. It
filleth my head with false security. Surely the government should care for me all the days of my life and I
shall dwell in a fool's paradise forever.

GRANDMOTHER

Just about the time a woman thinks her work is
done, she becomes a grandmother.

GRATITUDE

Next to ingratitude, the most painful thing
to bear is gratitude.
Henry Ward Beecher

He who receives a benefit with gratitude repays the
first installment on his debt.

GREATNESS

Keep away from people who try to belittle your
ambitions. Small people always do that, but the
really great make you feel that you, too,
can become great.
Mark Twain

To be great is to be misunderstood.

Emerson

Greatness lies not in being strong, but in
the right use of strength.

Henry Ward Beecher

I studied the lives of great men and famous
women, and I found that the men and women
who got to the top were those who did the
jobs they had in hand, with everything they had
of energy and enthusiasm and hard work.

Harry S. Truman

The greatest truths are the simplest—
and so are the greatest men.

Augustus Hare

There is a great person who makes every person feel
small. But the real great person is the person who
makes every person feel great.

G. K. Chesterton

GREED

One thing you can say for greed: It's responsible for
some imaginative rationalizations.

The weakness of this age is our inability to
distinguish our needs from our greeds.

GRIEF

Grief knits two hearts in closer bonds than happiness ever can; and common sufferings are far stronger links than common joys.

Lamartine

Where grief is fresh, any attempt to divert it only irritates.

Samuel Johnson

Grief can take care of itself, but to get the full value of a joy you must have somebody to divide it with.

Mark Twain

Nothing that grieves us can be called little: by the eternal laws of proportion a child's loss of a doll and a king's loss of a crown are events of the same size.

GROUCH

Grouches are nearly always pinheads, small men who have never made any effort to improve their mental capacity.

Thomas A. Edison

GROW UP

Is life so wretched? Isn't it rather your hands which are too small, your vision which is muddled? You are the one who must grow up.

Dag Hammarskjold

GROWING

Be not afraid of growing slowly, be afraid
only of standing still.

The strongest principle of growth lies
in human choice.

George Eliot

GROWING OLD

It takes some time to accept and realize the fact that
while you have been growing old, your friends have
not been standing still in that matter.

Don't resent growing old. A great many
are denied the privilege.

Reinbeck

GUESTS

After three days, fish and guests stink.

John Lyly

Unbidden guests are often welcomest
when they are gone.

William Shakespeare

GUILT

A guilty conscience is the mother of invention.

Carolyn Wells

Guilt is the gift that keeps on giving.

Erma Bombeck

HABIT

Reason stands small show against the
entrenched power of habit.

Elbert Hubbard

The mind unlearns with difficulty what it
has long learned.

Seneca

Habit, if not resisted, soon becomes necessity.

St. Augustine

The unfortunate thing about this world is that good
habits are so much easier to give up than bad ones.

Somerset Maugham

The best way to break a bad habit is to drop it.

D. S. Yoder

The chains of habit are weak to be felt until they are
too strong to be broken.
today than tomorrow.

HALF-WIT

The real wit tells jokes to make others feel superior,
while the half-wit tells them to make others feel small.

Elmer Wheeler

HAPPINESS

Happiness is not an end product in itself. It is a
by-product of working, playing, loving, and living.

Haim Ginott

Happiness? That's nothing more than health
and a poor memory.

Albert Schweitzer

What a wonderful life I've had! I only wish
I'd realized it sooner.

Colette

Happiness is not a state to arrive at, but a
manner of traveling.

Margaret Lee Runbeck

To be happy, add not to your possessions
but subtract from your desires.

Seneca

People will be happy in about the same
degree that they are helpful.

Happiness is a perfume which you can't
pour on someone without getting
some on yourself.

Emerson

There is only one way to happiness and that is
to cease worrying about things which are
beyond the power of our will.

Epictetus

Happiness is possible only when one is busy.

I have noticed that folks are generally about as happy
as they have made up their minds to be.

We are never so happy, nor so unhappy,
as we suppose ourselves to be.

Francois de La Rochefoucauld

It's pretty hard to tell what does bring happiness.
Poverty and wealth have both failed.

Kin Hubbard

Happiness is a butterfly, which when pursued is
always just beyond your grasp, but which, if you will
sit down quietly, may alight upon you.

Nathaniel Hawthorne

We are all happy if we only knew it.

Fodor Dostoyevski

Cherish all your happy moments: They make
a fine cushion for old age.

Christopher Morley

Never fear spoiling children by making them too happy. Happiness is the atmosphere in which all good affections grow.

Ann Eliza Bray

Happiness is your dentist telling you it won't hurt and then having him catch his hand in the drill.

Johnny Carson

Happiness consists of living each day as if it were the first day of your honeymoon and the last day of your vacation.

The Constitution only guarantees the American people the right to pursue happiness. You have to catch it yourself.

Benjamin Franklin

The really happy man is one who can enjoy the scenery on a detour.

HARD WORK

Hard work will not kill a man, but it almost scares some men to death.

HARVEST

Whatsoever a man soweth, that shall he also reap.

The Bible

HASTE

Make haste slowly.

Hasty climbers have sudden falls.

Haste makes waste.

God made time, but man made haste.

HATCHET

Nobody ever forgets where he buried a hatchet.
McKinney Frank Hubbard

HATE

It is better to eat soup with someone you love than steak with someone you hate.
The Bible

Hating people is like burning down your own home to get rid of a rat.
Harry Emerson Fosdick

Some persons, by hating vice too much, come to love men too little.

Hatred is self-punishment.

Hatred is the coward's revenge for being intimidated.
George Bernard Shaw

HEALTH

The poorest man would not part with health for money, but the richest would gladly part with all his money for health.
C. C. Colton

Quit worrying about your health. It'll go away.
Robert Orben

Those obsessed with health are not
healthy; the first requisite of good health is a
certain calculated carelessness about oneself.

Sydney J. Harris

There's lots of people in this world who spend so
much time watching their health that they
haven't the time to enjoy it.

Josh Billings

HEART

A happy face means a glad heart; a sad face
means a breaking heart.

The Bible

Where your treasure is, there will your
heart be also.

The Bible

Before we set our hearts too much on
anything, let us examine how happy are those
who already possess it.

Francois de La Rouchefoucauld

A glad heart makes a cheerful countenance . . .
a cheerful heart has a continual feast.

The Bible

HEARTBURN

I would like to find a stew that will give me
heartburn immediately, instead of at three
o'clock in the morning.

John Barrymore

HEAVEN

The good pastor said, "Nearly everyone is in favor
of going to heaven but too many are hoping
they'll live long enough to see an easing
of the entrance requirements."

Heaven goes by favor. If it went by merit, you
would stay out and your dog would go in.

Mark Twain

HELL

I never give them hell. I just tell the truth
and they think it's hell.

Harry S. Truman

It does not require a decision to go to hell.

The safest road to hell is the gradual one—the
gentle slope, soft underfoot, without sudden
turnings, without milestones, without signposts.

C. S. Lewis

Hell begins on the day when God grants us a clear
vision of all that we might have achieved, of all the
gifts which we have wasted, or all that we might
have done which we did not do. . . . For me the
conception of Hell lies in two words: Too Late.

Gian-Carlo Menotti

Hell is paved with good intentions.

St. Bernard

HELP

Sometimes nothing gives you a helping hand like
receiving a kick in the pants.

If you ever need a helping hand you'll find
one at the end of your arm.

You cannot help men permanently by doing for them
what they could and should do for themselves.
Abraham Lincoln

Down in their hearts, wise men know this truth: The
only way to help yourself is to help others.
Elbert Hubbard

You can't help a man uphill without getting closer
to the top yourself.

HEROES

Show me a hero and I will write you a tragedy.
F. Scott Fitzgerald

We can't all be heroes because someone has to sit
on the curb and clap as they go by.
Will Rogers

I've had several years in Hollywood and I still think
the movie heroes are in the audience.
Wilson Mizner

Being a hero is about the shortest-lived
profession on earth.
Will Rogers

Heroism consists in hanging on one minute longer.

HISTORY

Those who cannot remember the past are
condemned to repeat it.
George Santayana

Any event, once it has occurred, can be made to
appear inevitable by some competent historian.
Lee Simonson

History is the discovering of the constant and
universal principles of human nature.
David Hume

We Americans are the best informed people on earth
as to the events of the last 24 hours; we are not the
best informed as to the events of the last 60
centuries.
Ariel and Will Durant

When you read history it is quite astonishing to
discover that there never was a day when men
thought times were really good. Every generation in
history has been haunted by the feeling of crisis.
Harold Walker

It is not the neutrals or the lukewarms
who make history.
Adolf Hitler

HITLER

Hitler had the best answers to everything.
Charles Manson

HOLLYWOOD

Hollywood—a place where people from Iowa mistake each other for movie stars.

Fred Allen

Hollywood—a place where the inmates are in charge of the asylum.

Laurence Stallings

Strip away the phony tinsel of Hollywood and you fill find the real tinsel underneath.

Oscar Levant

Hollywood's a place where they'll pay you a thousand dollars for a kiss, and fifty cents for your soul.

Marilyn Monroe

Hollywood is where no one gives their right age, except in time of war.

In Hollywood, if you don't have a psychiatrist, people think you're crazy.

HOME

The number of accidents in the home is rising; people aren't spending enough time there to know their way around.

The strength of a nation is derived from the integrity of its homes.

Confucius

He is the happiest, be king or peasant,
who finds peace in his home.

Johann Wolfgang von Goethe

Home is a field where there may be grown
character, nobility, and song, or where by neglect
may grow the thorn tree of strife and
the bramble bush of discontent.

Mid pleasures and places though we may roam, be it
ever so humble, there's no place like home.

J. Howard Payne

Always leave home with a tender good-bye
and loving words. They may be the last.

HONESTY

Even a little lie is dangerous; it deteriorates the
conscience. And the importance of conscience
is eternal, like love.

Pablo Casals

There's one way to find out if a man is honest—ask
him. If he says, "Yes," you know he is a crook.

Groucho Marx

A man can build a staunch reputation for honesty
by admitting he was in error, especially
when he gets caught at it.

Robert Ruark

Honesty pays, but it don't seem to pay enough
to suit some people.

Kin Hubbard

No matter how brilliant a man may be, he will never engender confidence in his subordinates and associates if he lacks simple honesty and moral courage.

J. Lawton Collins

An honest man's the noblest work of God.

Alexander Pope

Honesty is the best policy.

Cervantes

HONEYMOON

Their honeymoon is over when he phones that he'll be late for supper and she has already left a note that it's in the refrigerator.

Bill Lawrence

HONOR

If somebody throws a brick at me, I can catch it and throw it back. But when somebody awards a decoration to me, I am out of words.

Harry S. Truman

It is better to deserve honors and not have them than to have them and not deserve them.

Mark Twain

HOPE

There is no medicine like hope, no incentive so great, and no tonic so powerful as expectation of something better tomorrow.

Orison Marden

Hope deferred makes the heart sick; but when
dreams come true at last, there is life and joy.
The Bible

Take from a man his wealth, and you hinder him;
take from him his purpose, and you slow him down.
But take from man his hope, and you stop him. He
can go on without wealth, and even without purpose,
for awhile. But he will not go on without hope.
C. Neil Strait

He who has health has hope. And he who
has hope has everything.

HORSE SENSE

The more horse sense a fellow has the
less he bets on 'em.
Kin Hubbard

Horse sense is what keeps horses from betting
on what people will do.
Raymond Nash

HOSPITAL

A hospital should also have a recovery room
adjoining the cashier's office.
Francis O'Walsh

HOSPITALITY

Hospitality is commended to be exercised, even
toward an enemy, when he cometh to thine house.
The tree does not withdraw its shadow, even
for the woodcutter.

It is equally offensive to speed a guest
who would like to stay and to detain
one who is anxious to leave.

Homer

HUMAN

To err is human, but when the eraser wears out
ahead of the pencil, you're overdoing it.

J. Jenkins

HUMAN BEING

The proof that the human being is the noblest of all
creatures is that no other creature has ever denied it.

Georg Christoph Lichtenberg

HUMAN NATURE

You can learn more about human nature by reading
the Bible than by living in New York.

William Lyon Phelps

HUMANITY

Human action can be modified to some extent, but
human nature cannot be changed.

Abraham Lincoln

We are always glad when a great man reassures us
of his humanity by possessing a few peculiarities.

André Maurois

HUMILITY

Be humble or you'll stumble.
Dwight L. Moody

The more humble a man is before God, the more he
will be exalted; the more humble he is before man,
the more he will get rode roughshod.
Josh Billings

Humility is to make a right estimate of one's self.
Charles H. Spurgeon

HUMOR

A well-developed sense of humor is the pole
that adds balance to your steps as you walk
the tightrope of life.
William A. Ward

If you could choose one characteristic that would get
you through life, choose a sense of humor.
Jennifer Jones

I think the next best thing to solving a problem is
finding some humor in it.
Frank A. Clark

A person without a sense of humor is like a wagon
without springs—jolted by every pebble in the road.
Henry Ward Beecher

Every survival kit should include a sense of humor.

When humor goes, there goes civilization.
Erma Bombeck

After God created the world, He made man and woman. Then, to keep the whole thing from collapsing, He invented humor.

Mack McGinnis

The secret source of humor is not joy but sorrow.

Mark Twain

Humor is an affirmation of dignity, a declaration of man's superiority to all that befalls him.

Romain Gary

HUNGER

It is a lot easier emotionally to handle the fact that millions of people are starving if we don't see them as individuals.

Stan Mooneyham

Hungry bellies have no ears.

Francois Rabelais

An empty stomach is not a good political adviser.

Albert Einstein

Hunger is the handmaid of genius.

Mark Twain

HURTS

It takes your enemy and your friend, working together, to hurt you to the heart; the one to slander you and the other to get the news to you.

Do we share our hurts or memorize them?

In this life we will encounter hurts and trials that we will not be able to change; we are just going to have to allow them to change us.

Ron Lee Davis

HUSBAND

An archaeologist is the best husband any woman can have: the older she gets, the more interested he is in her.

Agatha Christie

A good husband makes a good wife.

Some husbands know all the answers; they've been listening for years.

As the husband is, the wife is.

Tennyson

HYPOCRISY

Thou hypocrite, first cast out the beam out of thine own eye; and then shalt thou see clearly to cast out the mote out of thy brother's eye.

The Bible

A hypocrite is like the man who murdered both his parents and then pleaded for mercy on the grounds that he was an orphan.

Abraham Lincoln

IDEALISM

Idealism increases in direct proportion to
one's distance from the problem.

John Galsworthy

IDEAS

With no ideas of diamonds, we settle for glass.

Ideas are funny things. They don't work
unless you do.

The ideas I stand for are not mine. I borrowed them
from Socrates. I swiped them from Chesterfield. I
stole them from Jesus. And I put them in a book. If
you don't like their rules, whose would you use?

Dale Carnegie

There is one thing stronger than all the armies in the
world: and that is an idea whose time has come.

Victor Hugo

Sometimes a person's mind is stretched by a new idea and never does go back to its old dimensions.
Oliver Wendell Holmes

Almost all really new ideas have a certain aspect of foolishness when they are first produced.
Alfred North Whitehead

A new idea is delicate. It can be killed by a sneer or a yawn; it can be stabbed to death by a quip and worried to death by a frown on the right man's brow.
Charles Brower

It's tough watching a good idea lose because its backers are less eloquent or have less clout than its opponents.
Lester Case

Ideas are like children—no matter how much you admire someone else's you can't help liking your own best.

He objected to ideas only when others had them.
A. J. P. Taylor

IDLE

Idle folks have the least leisure.

Idle folks lack no excuses.

People who have nothing to do are quickly tired of their own company.
Collier

The man with time to burn never gave the world any light.

An idle brain is the devil's workshop.

Prolonged idleness paralyzes initiative.

No one has a right to live in idleness and expect to live long and be happy. The ship anchored in the harbor rots faster than the ship crossing the ocean; a still pond of water stagnates more rapidly than a running stream. Our unused minds are subject to atrophy much more rapidly than those in use. The unused cells in our brains deteriorate much faster than those which are continually exercised. Hence, to remain young we must remain active.

IGNORANCE

You can say one thing for ignorance—it certainly causes a lot of interesting arguments.

Ignorance is never out of style. It was in fashion yesterday, it is the rage today, and it will set the pace tomorrow.

Frank Dane

The older we grow the greater becomes our wonder at how much ignorance one can contain without bursting one's clothes.

Mark Twain

I have never met a man so ignorant that I couldn't learn something from him.

Galileo Galilei

When I was a boy of fourteen, my father was so ignorant I could hardly stand to have the old man around. But when I got to be twenty-one, I was astonished at how much the old man had learned.

Mark Twain

Everyone is ignorant, only on different subjects.

Will Rogers

ILLNESS

The doctor may also learn more about the illness from the way the patient tells the story than from the story itself.

James B. Herrick

ILLUSTRATIONS

The sermon is the house; the illustrations are the windows that let in the light.

Charles H. Spurgeon

IMAGINATION

When you stop having dreams and ideals—well, you might as well stop altogether.

There's no better way of exercising the imagination than the study of law. No poet ever interpreted nature as freely as a lawyer interprets truth.

IMITATION

Imitation is the sincerest form of flattery.

IMPOSSIBLE

The difficult we do immediately, the impossible takes a little longer.

You can't get blood out of a turnip.

You can't make a silk purse out of a sow's ear.

INCOME

I'm living so far beyond my income that we may almost be said to be living apart.

Hector Munro

Live within your income, even if you have to borrow money to do so.

Josh Billings

INCOME TAX

Income-tax forms should be more realistic by allowing the taxpayer to list Uncle Sam as a dependent.

INCOMPATIBILITY

A little incompatibility is the spice of life, particularly if he has income and she is pattable.

Ogden Nash

INDECISION

Don't stand shivering upon the bank; plunge in at once, and have it over.

Sam Slick

On the Plains of Hesitation bleach the bones of countless millions who, at the Dawn of Victory, sat down to
wait—and waiting, died.

George W. Cecil

INDIVIDUALITY

Resolve to be thyself; and know that he who finds
himself loses his misery.

Matthew Arnold

INDULGENCE

Do you like honey? Don't eat too much of it, or it
will make you sick!

The Bible

INDUSTRY

In the ordinary business of life, industry can do
anything which genius can do, and very many
things which it cannot.

Henry Ward Beecher

The bread earned by the sweat of the brow is
thrice blessed bread, and it is far sweeter than the
tasteless loaf of idleness.

Whatsoever thy hand findeth to do, do it
with all thy might.

The Bible

Elbow grease gives the best polish.

Like the bee, we should make our industry
our amusement.

Oliver Goldsmith

A man who gives his children habits of industry
provides for them better than by
giving them a fortune.

Richard Whately

INFERIORITY

No one can make you feel inferior without
your consent.

Eleanore Roosevelt

No man who says, "I'm as good as you," believes it.
He would not say it if he did. The Saint Bernard
never says it to the toy dog, nor the scholar to the
dunce, nor the employable to the bum, nor the pretty
woman to the plain. The claim to equality is made
only by those who feel themselves to be in some
way inferior. What it expresses is the itching,
smarting awareness of an inferiority which the
patient refuses to accept. And therefore resents.

C. S. Lewis

INFLATION

Try to save money. Someday it may be
valuable again.

At today's prices you can hardly
make one end meet.

One thing is true, people are certainly getting stronger. Ten years ago it took two people to carry ten dollars worth of groceries. Today, a child can do it.

Ronald Reagan

Inflation is when you want to pay cash for something and they ask for two pieces of identification.

INFLUENCE

Ten persons who speak make more noise than 10,000 who are silent.

Napoleon Bonaparte

Say it simple. Say it often. Make it burn.

Adolf Hitler

The best way for a young man who is without friends or influence to begin is: first, to get a position; second, to keep his mouth shut; third, observe; fourth, be faithful; fifth, make his employer think he would be lost in a fog without him; sixth, be polite.

Russell Sage

INGRATITUDE

Ingratitude is always a form of weakness. I have never known a man of real ability to be ungrateful.

Johann Wolfgang von Goethe

INHERITANCE

We pay for the mistakes of our ancestors, and it
seems only fair that they should leave us the
money to pay with.

Don Marquis

INITIATIVE

The men who try to do something and fail are
infinitely better than those who try to do nothing
and succeed.

Lloyd Jones

INJURIES

The injuries we do and those we suffer are seldom
weighed on the same scales.

Aesop

INJUSTICE

He who commits injustice is ever made more
wretched than he who suffers it.

Plato

INSANITY

Insanity is hereditary; you can get it
from your children.

Sam Levenson

Though this be madness, yet there is a method in it.

William Shakespeare

INSECTS

When the insects take over the world we hope they will remember, with gratitude, how we took them along on our picnics.

Bill Vaughn

INSPIRATION

I don't know anything about inspiration because I don't know what inspiration is; I've heard about it, but I never saw it.

William Faulkner

INSTITUTION

An institution is the lengthened shadow of one man.

Emerson

INSULT

The only graceful way to accept an insult is to ignore it; if you can't ignore it, top it; if you can't top it, laugh at it; if you can't laugh at it, it's probably deserved.

Russell Lynes

The way to procure insults is to submit to them. A man meets with no more respect than he exacts.

William Hazlitt

It is often better not to see an insult than to avenge it.

Seneca

INTEGRITY

Better be poor and honest than rich and dishonest.
The Bible

Few men have virtue to withstand
the highest bidder.
George Washington

INTELLIGENCE

I've always felt that a person's intelligence is directly
reflected by the number of conflicting points of view
he can entertain simultaneously on the same topic.
Lisa Alther

INTOLERANCE

The devil loves nothing better than the
intolerance of reformers.
Abbott Lowell

I hate intolerant people.

INTRODUCTIONS

Early in his career as a lecturer, Mark Twain grew so
vexed with the bumbling introductions he received
from local leaders that he resolved to do away with
formal introductions altogether and introduce himself.
One of the introductions he received which settled
him on this policy came from a miner who was
nominated to introduce Mark Twain to a Nevada
audience. The miner, who was unaccustomed to
public speaking, introduced Twain with these words:

"I don't know anything about this man. Anyhow, I only know two things about him. One is, he has never been in jail. And the other is, I don't know why."

INTRUSIVENESS

The great secret of life is never to be in the way of others.

Haliburton

INVENTION

If a man can write a better book, or preach a better sermon, or build a better mousetrap than his neighbor, though he builds his house in the woods, the world will make a beaten path to his door.

Emerson

I don't think necessity is the mother of invention. Invention, in my opinion, arises directly from idleness, possibly also from laziness— to save oneself trouble.

Agatha Christie

INVENTOR

I invent nothing. I rediscover.

Auguste Rodin

INVOLVEMENT

Plunge boldly into the thick of life!

Johann Wolfgang von Goethe

IRON RULE

While my mother believes in the Golden Rule, she
also advocates a second maxim, which she terms
her Iron Rule: "Don't do for others what they
wouldn't take the trouble to do for themselves."

Mrs. D. Fulton

IRS

April showers are the tears shed over taxes
paid to the IRS.

JEALOUSY

In jealousy there is more self-love than love.

Francois de La Rochefoucauld

The jealous are troublesome to others, but a
torment to themselves.

William Penn

Jealousy is the dragon in paradise; the hell of heaven;
and the most bitter of the emotions because
associated with the sweetest.

A. R. Orage

JEST

He that would jest must take a jest,
else to let it alone were best.

Many a true word is spoke in jest.

JESUS CHRIST

Philosophical argument has sometimes shaken my
reason for the faith that was in me; but my heart
has always assured me that the Gospel
of Jesus Christ must be reality.

Daniel Webster

Alexander, Caesar, Charlemagne, and myself found
empires; but on what foundation did we rest the
creations of our genius? Upon Force. Jesus Christ
founded an empire upon love; and at this hour
millions of men would die for Him.

Napoleon Bonaparte

It takes no brains to be an atheist. Any stupid
person can deny the existence of a supernatural
power because man's physical senses cannot
detect it. But here cannot be ignored the influence
of conscience, the respect we feel for moral law, the
mystery of first life . . . or the marvelous order in
which the universe moves about us on this earth.
All these evidence the handiwork of the beneficent
Deity. For my part that Deity is the God of the Bible
and of Jesus Christ, His Son.

Dwight D. Eisenhower

Of all the systems of morality, ancient or modern
which have come under my observation, none
appear to me so pure as that of Jesus.

Thomas Jefferson

JOKE

A joke that has to be explained is at its wit's end.

Jokes of the proper kind, properly told, can do more to enlighten questions of politics, philosophy, and literature than any number of dull arguments.
Isaac Asimov

Were it not for my little jokes, I could not bear the burdens of this office.
Abraham Lincoln

I don't make jokes. I just watch the government and report the facts.
Will Rogers

JOURNALISM

Doctors bury their mistakes. Lawyers hang theirs. And journalists put theirs on the front page.

The men with the muckrakes are often indispensable to the well-being of society; but only if they know when to stop raking the muck, and look upward to the celestial crown above them, the crown of worthy endeavor. There are beautiful things above and round about them; and if they gradually grow to feel that the whole world is nothing but muck, their power of usefulness is gone.
Theodore Roosevelt

I have yet to see a piece of writing, political or non-political, that doesn't have a slant. All writing slants the way a writer leans, and no man is born perpendicular, although many men are born upright. The beauty of the American free press is that the slants and the twists and the distortions come from so many directions, and the special interests are so numerous, the

reader must sift and sort and check and
countercheck in order to find out
what the score is.

E. B. White

JOY

One joy dispels a hundred cares.

JUDGING

We are all inclined to judge ourselves by our
ideals, others by their acts.

Harold Nicholson

Before I judge my neighbor, let me walk a
mile in his moccasins.

Judge a tree from its fruit; not from the leaves.

Euripides

Examine the contents, not the bottle.

The Talmud

Judge a man by his questions rather than
by his answers.

Voltaire

Four things belong to a judge: to hear courteously,
to answer wisely, to consider soberly, and
to decide impartially.

Socrates

Never be a judge between thy friends in any matter
where both set their hearts upon the victory. If

strangers or enemies be litigants, whatever side thou favorest, thou gettest a friend, but when friends are the parties thou losest one.

Jeremy Taylor

If you judge people, you have no time to love them.

Mother Teresa

JUDGMENT

One man's word is no man's word; we should quietly hear both sides.

Johann Wolfgang von Goethe

Give your decision, never your reasons; your decisions may be right, your reasons are sure to be wrong.

Lord Mansfield

Every man prefers belief to the exercise of judgment.

Seneca

Good judgment comes from experience; and experience, well, that comes from bad judgment.

JUNK

Junk is something you keep for years and then throw out two weeks before you need it.

JURY

A fox should not be the jury at a goose's trial.

Thomas Fuller

A jury consists of twelve persons chosen to decide who has the better lawyer.

Robert Frost

JUSTICE

Justice is truth in action.

Joubert

Justice without force is powerless; force without justice is tyrannical.

Blaise Pascal

Justice discards party, friendship, kindred, and is always, therefore, represented as blind.

Joseph Addison

Injustice is relatively easy to bear; what stings is justice.

H. L. Mencken

Man's capacity for justice makes democracy possible; but man's inclination to injustice makes democracy necessary.

Reinhold Niebuhr

KINDNESS

Constant kindness can accomplish much.
As the sun makes ice melt, kindness causes
misunderstanding, mistrust, and hostility
to evaporate.

Albert Schweitzer

Never tire of loyalty and kindness. Hold these
virtues tightly. Write them deep within your heart.

The Bible

Wise sayings often fall on barren ground; but a kind
word is never thrown away.

Sir Arthur Helps

Kindness has converted more sinners than zeal,
eloquence, or learning.

Frederick W. Faber

Kindness makes a fellow feel good whether
it's being done to him or by him.

Frank A. Clark

One can pay back the loan of gold, but one lies forever in debt to those who are kind.

One kind word can warm three winter months.

Kindness is irresistible, be it but sincere and no mock smile or mask assumed. For what can the most unconscionable of men do to thee if thou persist in being kindly to him?

Marcus Aurelius

To speak kindly does not hurt the tongue.

The greatness of a man can nearly always be measured by his willingness to be kind.

G. Young

KISS

Some women blush when they are kissed; some call for the police, some swear; some bite. But the worst are those who laugh.

KNOWLEDGE

All knowledge has its origins in our perceptions.

Leonardo da Vinci

Since we cannot know all that is to be known of everything, we ought to know a little about everything.

Blaise Pascal

We do not know one-millionth of one percent about anything.

Thomas A. Edison

Some students drink at the fountain of knowledge. Others just gargle.

Those who think they know it all are very annoying to those of us who do.

Robert K. Mueller

The trouble with the world is not that people know too little, but that they know so many things that ain't so.

Mark Twain

Strange how much you've got to know before you know how little you know.

Universities are full of knowledge; the freshmen bring a little in and the seniors take none away, and knowledge accumulates.

Abbott Lowell

The less we know the more we suspect.

H. W. Shaw

LABOR

If you wish to be at rest, labor.
Brother Giles of Assisi

Thank God every morning when you get up
that you have something to do that day which must
be done, whether you like it or not. Being forced to
work, and forced to do your best, will breed in you
temperance and self-control, diligence and strength of
will, cheerfulness and content, and a hundred virtues
which the idle never know.
Charles Kingsley

If a man love the labor of any trade apart from
any question of success or fame,
the gods have called him.
Robert Louis Stevenson

LANGUAGE

The chief virtue that language can have is
clearness, and nothing detracts from it

so much as the use of
unfamiliar words.

Hippocrates

Drawing on my fine command of language,
I said nothing.

Robert Benchley

Our language is funny—a fat chance and
slim chance are the same thing.

J. Gustav White

LAUGHTER

Man is the only animal that laughs and has a
state legislature.

Samuel Butler

To laugh often and much; to win respect of intelligent
people and affection of children . . . to leave the
world a better place . . . to know even one life has
breathed easier because you have lived. This is to
have succeeded.

Emerson

If you wish to glimpse inside a human soul and get
to know a man, don't bother analyzing his ways
of being silent, of talking, of weeping, of seeing
how much he is moved by noble ideas; you will
get better results if you just watch him laugh.
If he laughs well, he's a good man.

Fyodor Dostoyevski

We must laugh at man, to avoid crying for him.

Napoleon Bonaparte

Sexiness wears thin after a while and beauty fades, but to be married to a man who makes you laugh every day, ah, now that's a real treat!

Joanne Woodward

A hearty laugh gives one a dry cleaning, while a good cry is a wet wash.

If you're not allowed to laugh in heaven, I don't want to go there.

Martin Luther

A good laugh is sunshine in a house.

William Thackeray

Of all the things God created, I am often most grateful He created laughter.

Charles Swindoll

He who has learned how to laugh at himself shall never cease to be entertained.

John Powell

He who laughs, lasts.

Mary Pettibone Poole

If any cleric or monk speaks jocular words, such as provoke laughter, let him be anathema.

Ordinance, Second Council of Constance (1418)

With the fearful strain that is on me night and day, if I did not laugh I should die.

Abraham Lincoln

Laughter is the shortest distance
between two people.

Victor Borge

LAW

Laws too gentle are seldom obeyed;
too severe, seldom executed.

Benjamin Franklin

We must reject the idea that every time a law is
broken, society is guilty rather than the lawbreaker.
It is time to restore the American precept that each
individual is accountable for his actions.

Ronald Reagan

To succeed in the other trades, capacity must be
shown; in the law, concealment of it will do.

LAWSUIT

Lawsuit: A machine which you go into as a
pig and come out as a sausage.

Ambrose Bierce

LAWYER

A poor man between two lawyers is like a
fish between two cats.

As well open an oyster without a knife, as a
lawyer's mouth without a fee.

A lawyer is someone who helps you get what
is coming to him.

Lawyers spend a great deal of their time
shoveling smoke.

Oliver Wendell Holmes

The first thing we do, let's kill all the lawyers.

William Shakespeare

Anybody who thinks talk is cheap should get
some legal advice.

Franklin P. Jones

The houses of lawyers are roofed with the
skins of litigants.

The lawyers have twisted it into such a state of
bedevilment that the original merits of the case have
long disappeared from the face of the earth. It's
about a Will, and the trusts under a Will—or it was
once. It's about nothing but Costs now.

Charles Dickens

LAZINESS

To do nothing is in every man's power.

Samuel Johnson

Laziness grows on people; it begins in cobwebs
and ends in iron chains.

M. Hale

Laziness travels so slowly that poverty
soon overtakes him.

Take a lesson from the ants, you lazy fellow. Learn from their ways and be wise! For though they have no king to make them work, yet they labor hard all summer, gathering food for the winter. But you—all you do is sleep. When will you wake up?

The Bible

LEADERSHIP

The supreme quality for leadership is unquestionably integrity. Without it, no real success is possible, no matter whether it is on a section gang, a football field, in an army, or in an office.

Dwight D. Eisenhower

Some must follow, and some command, though all are made of clay.

Henry Wadsworth Longfellow

You do not lead by hitting people over the head— that's assault, not leadership.

Dwight D. Eisenhower

No man will ever be a big executive who feels that he must, either openly or under cover, follow up every order he gives and see that it is done—nor will he ever develop a capable assistant.

John L. Mahin

You can judge a leader by the size of the problems he tackles—people nearly always pick a problem their own size, and ignore or leave to others the bigger or smaller ones.

Anthony Jay

Anyone can steer the ship when the sea is calm.

Publilius Syrus

He who cannot obey, cannot command.

Benjamin Franklin

The penalty of leadership is loneliness.

H. Wheeler Robinson

When you soar like an eagle, you
attract hunters.

Milton S. Gould

LEARNING

Men learn while they teach.

Seneca

Wear your learning like your watch, in a private
pocket; and do not pull it out and strike it, merely to
show that you have one.

Lord Chesterfield

The three foundations of learning: seeing much,
suffering much, and studying much.

Caterall

LEISURE

The real problem with your leisure is how to
keep other people from using it.

Leisure is the mother of philosophy.

Thomas Hobbes

LETTER

I have made this letter longer than usual because I lack the time to make it shorter.

Blaise Pascal

When a man sends you an impudent letter, sit right down and give it back to him with interest ten times compounded—and then throw both letters in the wastebasket.

Elbert Hubbard

LIAR

A liar needs a good memory.

Quintilian

The biggest liar in the world is—"They Say."

Douglas Malloch

The liar's punishment is not in the least that he is not believed but that he cannot believe anyone else.

George Bernard Shaw

No man has good enough memory to be a successful liar.

Abraham Lincoln

LIBERAL

I can remember way back when a liberal was one who was generous with his own money.

Will Rogers

A liberal: One who has both feet firmly
planted in the air.

It really shakes you to see one of the liberal
congressmen sign a piece of legislation, and then
wipe their fingerprints off the pen.

For the average American, the message is clear.
Liberalism is no longer the answer. It is the problem.

Ronald Reagan

The trend of democracy is toward socialism,
while the Republican party stands for a wise and
regulated individualism. Socialism would destroy
wealth; Republicanism would prevent its abuse.
Socialism would give to each an equal right to take;
Republicanism would give to each an equal right to
earn. Socialism would offer an equality of
possession which would soon leave no one
anything to possess; Republicanism would give
equality of opportunity.

Republican Party Platform

You know what they say: If God had been a liberal,
we wouldn't have the Ten Commandments. We'd
have the ten suggestions.

Malcolm Bradbury

The liberals can understand everything but people
who don't understand them.

LIBERTY

Liberty is the only thing you cannot have
unless you are willing to give
it to others.

William Allen White

When liberty destroys order, the hunger for order will destroy liberty.

Will Durant

Let every nation know, whether it wishes us well or ill, that we shall pay any price, bear any burden, meet any hardship, support any friend, oppose any foe, in order to assure the survival and the success of liberty.

John F. Kennedy

We who lived in concentration camps can remember the men who walked through the huts comforting others, giving away their last piece of bread. They may have been few in number, but they offer sufficient proof that everything can be taken from a man but one thing: the last of human freedoms—to choose one's attitude in any given set of circumstances—to choose one's own way.

Viktor Frankl

When you have robbed a man of everything, he is no longer in your power. He is free again.

Alexander Solzhenitsyn

We are in bondage to the law in order that we may be free.

Cicero

Eternal vigilance is the price of liberty.

W. Phillips

Liberty means responsibility. That is why most men dread it.

George Bernard Shaw

He that would make his own liberty secure must guard even his enemy from oppression.

Thomas Paine

Give me liberty, or give me death.

Patrick Henry

The ground of liberty must be gained by inches.

Thomas Jefferson

Liberty, when it begins to take root, is a plant of rapid growth.

George Washington

Liberty has never come from the government. Liberty has always come from the subjects of it. The history of liberty is a history of resistance. The history of liberty is a history of limitations of governmental power, not the increase of it.

Woodrow Wilson

LIES

Telling lies about someone is as harmful as hitting him with an axe, or wounding him with a sword, or shooting him with a sharp arrow.

The Bible

The cruelest lies are often told in silence.

Robert Louis Stevenson

One of the striking differences between a cat and a lie is that the cat has only nine lives.

Mark Twain

Those that think it permissible to tell white lies
soon grow color-blind.

Austin O'Malley

LIFE

Life not only begins at forty—it begins to show.

The first half of our life is ruined by our parents and
the second half by our children.

Clarence Darrow

Life would be infinitely happier if we could only
be born at the age of eighty and gradually
approach eighteen.

Mark Twain

The trouble with life is that it is so daily.

We are always complaining that our days are few,
and acting as though there would be no end to them.

Seneca

Life is easier to take than you'd think; all that is
necessary is to accept the impossible, do without the
indispensable, and bear the intolerable.

Kathleen Norris

Live each day as if it were your last—
someday you'll be right.

As is a tale, so is life: not how long it is, but how good it is, is what matters.

Seneca

The great use of life is to spend it for something that outlasts it.

William James

Life is what we make it, always has been, always will be.

Grandma Moses

The main dangers in this life are the people who want to change everything . . . or nothing.

Lady Nancy Astor

A life of ease is a difficult pursuit.

William Cowper

Life consists not in holding good cards, but in playing well those you do hold.

Josh Billings

I expect to pass through life but once. If therefore, there can be any kindness I can show, or any good thing I can do to any fellow being, let me do it now, and not defer or neglect it, as I shall not pass this way again.

William Penn

Life is not so short but that there is always time enough for courtesy.

Emerson

LIGHT

Better to light one small candle
than to curse the darkness.

We are told to let our light shine, and if it does,
we won't need to tell anybody it does. Lighthouses
don't fire cannons to call attention to their
shining—they just shine.

D. L. Moody

LINCOLN

His heart was as great as the world, but there was no
room in it to hold the memory of a wrong.

Emerson

LISTENING

It takes a great man to make a good listener.

Sir Arthur Helps

No man would listen to you talk if he didn't know it
was his turn next.

Edgar Watson Howe

People will listen a great deal more
patiently while you explain your mistakes
than when you explain
your successes.

Wilbur N. Nesbit

One cardinal rule: One must always
listen to the patient.

Dr. Oliver

A good listener is not only popular everywhere,
but after a while he knows something.
Wilson Mizner

What a shame—yes, how stupid!—to decide
before knowing the facts!
The Bible

One of the best ways to persuade others
is by listening to them.
Dean Rusk

When a woman is speaking to you, listen to what
she says with her eyes.
Victor Hugo

LITERATURE

In literature as in love, we are astonished at
what is chosen by others.
Andre Maurois

The great standard of literature as to purity
and exactness of style is the Bible.
Hugh Blair

Read it aloud. I may be wrong, still it is my
conviction that one cannot get out of finely
wrought literature all that is in it by reading it mutely.
William Dean Howells

LITTLE THINGS

It isn't the mountains ahead that wear you out.

It's the grain of sand in your shoe.

LOGIC

Logic is like the sword—those who appeal to
it shall perish by it.

Samuel Butler

Against logic there is no armor like ignorance.

Lawrence J. Peter

If you're strong on facts and weak on logic, talk facts;
if you're strong on logic and weak on facts, talk logic.
If you're weak on both, pound on the table.

LONELINESS

It is strange to be known so universally
and yet to be so lonely.

Albert Einstein

He must start for the pole. In plain words, he must
face the loneliness of original work. No one can cut
new paths in company. He does that alone.

Oliver Wendell Holmes

The best remedy for those who are afraid, lonely, or
unhappy is to go outside, somewhere where they
can be quite alone with the heavens, nature, and
God. Because only then does one feel that all is as it
should be and that God wishes to see people happy
amidst the simple beauty of nature.

Anne Frank

Always have some project under way . . . an ongoing project that goes over from day to day and thus makes each day a smaller unit of time.

Lillian Troll

Get out of the house every day. Rain, shine, or snow, be sure to stay out at least two or three hours and meet people of all ages.

Michael Vaught

LORD'S PRAYER

Do you wish to see that which is really sublime? Repeat the Lord's Prayer.

Napoleon Bonaparte

LOSERS

He's a real loser. He moved into a new neighborhood and got run over by the Welcome Wagon.

Red Buttons

LOVE

Nothing raises man to such noble peaks nor drops him into such ashpits of absurdity as the act of falling in love.

Ridgely Hunt

If Jack's in love, he's no judge of Jill's beauty.

Benjamin Franklin

Love is friendship set on fire.

Jeremy Taylor

Love does not die easily. It is a living thing.
It thrives in the face of all life's hazards,
save one—neglect.

James Bryden

Love will always find a way to be practical.

Joe White

I love mankind—it's people I can't stand!

Linus

Love: A grave mental illness.

Plato

The heart has its reasons which reason
does not understand.

Blaise Pascal

The way to a man's heart is through
his stomach.

Love never dies of starvation but often
of indigestion.

Ninon de Lenclos

Love is the only fire against which there
is no insurance.

Love is blind—and marriage is an eye-opener.

Love cures people—both the ones who give it
and the ones who receive it.

Karl Menninger

In life, actions speak louder than words, but
in love, the eyes do.
Susan B. Anthony

If you would be loved, be lovable.
Benjamin Franklin

The way to love anything is to realize
that it might be lost.
G. K. Chesterton

Love is a softening of the hearteries.

An old man in love is like a flower in winter.

The heart that loves is always young.

Where there is great love there is great pain.

There is no fear in love; but perfect love
casteth out fear.
The Bible

Greater love hath no man than this, that a
man lay down his life for his friends.
The Bible

Love sought is good, but given unsought is better.
William Shakespeare

Some pray to marry the man they love, my prayer
will somewhat vary: I humbly pray to heaven above
that I love the man I marry.
Rose Pastor Stokes

Love is very patient and kind, never jealous or
envious, never boastful or proud, never haughty or

selfish or rude. Love does not demand its own way.
It is not irritable or touchy. It does not hold grudges
and will hardly even notice when others do it wrong.
It is never glad about injustice, but rejoices whenever
truth wins out. If you love someone you will be loyal
to him no matter what the cost. You will always
believe in him, always expect the best of him, and
always stand your ground in defending him.

The Bible

There are three things that remain—faith, hope, and
love—and the greatest of these is love.

The Bible

Love seems the swiftest, but it is the slowest of all
growths. No man or woman really knows
what perfect love is until they have been married
a quarter of a century.

Mark Twain

If you hear bells, get your ears checked.

Erich Segal

Love is a fruit in season at all times, and within
reach of every hand.

Mother Teresa

Love looks through a telescope; envy,
through a microscope.

LOYALTY

We are all in the same boat in a stormy sea,
and we owe each other a terrible loyalty.

G. K. Chesterton

It is better to be faithful than famous.
Theodore Roosevelt

Often loyalty consists of keeping your mouth shut.

LUCK

I'm a great believer in luck and I find the harder I work the more I have of it.
Stephen Leacock

MAD

Man is certainly stark mad; he cannot make a worm,
and yet he will be making gods by dozens.

Michel de Montaigne

When you see a married couple coming down
the street, the one who is two or three steps
ahead is the one that's mad.

Helen Rowland

MALICE

Malice drinks its own poison.

With malice toward none, with charity
for all, with firmness in the right, as God

gives us to see the right.

Abraham Lincoln

MAN

Man is a prisoner who has no right to open the
door of his prison and run away. . . . A man
should wait, and not take his own life
until God summons him.

Plato

Men are the only animals that devote themselves,
day in and day out, to making one another unhappy.

H. L. Mencken

All I care to know is that a man is a human
being—that is enough for me; he can't be any worse.

Mark Twain

MANAGEMENT

So much of what we call management consists in
making it difficult for people to work.

Peter Drucker

MANNERS

Manners are the happy ways of doing things.

Emerson

One learns manners from those who have none.

Self-respect is at the bottom of all good manners.
They are the expression of discipline,
of goodwill, of respect for other people's rights
and comforts and feelings.

Edward S. Martin

MANUSCRIPT

A manuscript, like a fetus, is never improved by
showing it to somebody before it is completed.

Your manuscript is both good and original; but the
part that is good is not original, and the part that is
original is not good.

Samuel Johnson

Manuscript: Something submitted in haste
and returned at leisure.

Oliver Herford

MARRIAGE

Often the difference between a successful marriage
and a mediocre one consists of leaving about three
or four things a day unsaid.

Harlan Miller

To keep your marriage brimming,
With love in the loving cup,
Whenever you're wrong, admit it,
Whenever you're right, shut up.

Ogden Nash

I have done thousands of hours of marriage
counseling and, yet, I have never seen two
unselfish people ever get a divorce. I never
have had anyone rush into my office and say,
"I want out of this marriage. My spouse has
been too good and too nice to me."

R. E. Phillips

Keep thy eyes wide open before marriage,
and half shut afterward.

Thomas Fuller

A good marriage would be between a blind wife
and a deaf husband.

Michel de Montaigne

Marriage means expectations and
expectations mean conflict.

Anthony Clare

Better to sit up all night than to go to bed
with a dragon.

Jeremy Taylor

The goal of our life should not be to find joy in
marriage, but to bring more love and truth into the
world. We marry to assist each other in this task.
The most selfish and hateful life of all is that of two
beings who unite in order to enjoy life. The highest
calling is that of the man who has dedicated his life
to serving God and doing good, and who unites with
a woman in order to further that purpose.

Leo Tolstoy

A successful marriage is one in which
you fall in love many times, always
with the same person.

Mignon McLaughlin

It is not marriage that fails; it is people
that fail. All that marriage does is to
show people up.

Harry Emerson Fosdick

If love means never having to say
you're sorry, then marriage means always
having to say everything twice.
Estelle Getty

Husband and wife come to look alike at last.
Oliver Wendell Holmes

When a girl marries she exchanges the
attentions of many men
for the inattention of one.
Helen Rowland

MARTYR

The tyrant dies and his rule ends, the martyr
dies and his rule begins.
Soren Kierkegaard

The blood of the martyrs is the seed of the church.
Tertullian

MATURITY

At sixteen I was stupid, confused, insecure, and
indecisive. At twenty-five I was wise, self-confident,
prepossessing, and assertive. At forty-five I am
stupid, confused, insecure, and indecisive. Who
would have supposed that maturity is only a short
break in adolescence?
Jules Feiffer

Maturity is: the ability to stick with a job until it's
finished; the ability to do a job without being
supervised; the ability to carry money without

spending it; and the ability to bear an injustice without wanting to get even.

Abigail Van Buren

MEMORIES

God gave us our memories so that we might have roses in December.

James Barrie

Let us not burden our remembrances with a heaviness that is gone.

William Shakespeare

When waiting for old age, be sure to put away a few pleasant thoughts.

Why can we remember the tiniest detail that has happened to us, and not remember how many times we have told it to the same persons?

Francois de La Rochefoucauld

The creditor hath a better memory than the debtor.

James Howell

MEMORY

A retentive memory is a good thing, but the ability to forget is the true token of greatness.

Elbert Hubbard

When I was younger I could remember anything, whether it had happened or not.

Mark Twain

Everyone complains about his memory, and no one complains about his judgment.

Francois de La Rochefoucauld

He who is not very strong in memory should not meddle with lying.

Michel de Montaigne

I used to have trouble remembering names till I took that Sam Carnegie course.

Jack Taylor

You never realize what a good memory you have until you try to forget something.

MEN

An important difference between men and women is that women are smarter than men about women.

God give us men. A time like this demands strong minds, great hearts, true faith, and ready hands! Men whom the lust of office does not kill, men whom the spoils of office cannot buy, men who possess opinions and a will, men who love honor, men who cannot lie.

J. G. Holland

MIDDLE AGE

Middle age is when your age starts to show around your middle.

Bob Hope

Middle age is when you're sitting at home on Saturday night and the telephone rings and you hope it isn't for you.

Ogden Nash

Middle age is when your old classmates are so grey and wrinkled and bald they don't recognize you.

Bennet Cerf

Life begins at forty—but so do fallen arches, lumbago, faulty eyesight, and the tendency to tell a story to the same person three or four times.

Bill Feather

You've reached middle age when people begin to recognize you from the rear too.

Middle age is when everything starts to click—your elbows, knees, and neck.

Robert Orben

Middle age is when your narrow waist and broad mind begin to change places.

Ben Klitzner

The really frightening thing about middle age is the knowledge that you'll grow out of it.

Doris Day

MIGHT

It has been said of the world's history hitherto that might makes right. It is for us and for our time to reverse the maxim, and to say that right makes might.

Abraham Lincoln

MINORITIES

The only tyrannies from which men, women,
and children are suffering in real life are the
tyrannies of minorities.

Theodore Roosevelt

MIRACLE

A modern-day miracle would be a golden wedding
anniversary in Hollywood.

MISCOMMUNICATION

All miscommunication is the result of
differing assumptions.

MISER

Misers aren't fun to live with, but they make
wonderful ancestors.

David Brenner

MISERABLE

The secret of being miserable is to have the leisure
to bother about whether you are happy or not.

George Bernard Shaw

Misery loves company.
Fire tries gold, misery tries brave men.

Seneca

He that is down need fear no fall.

John Bunyan

MISFORTUNE

If all our misfortunes were laid in one common
heap, whence everyone must take an equal portion,
most people would be contented to take
their own and depart.

Solon

Great minds have purposes, others have wishes.
Little minds are tamed and subdued by misfortune;
but great minds rise above them.

Washington Irving

The measure of a man is the way he bears
up under misfortune.

Plutarch

Let us be of good cheer, remembering
that the misfortunes hardest to bear are those
which never happen.

James Russell Lowell

MISTAKE

A mistake at least proves somebody stopped
talking long enough to do something.

A man who refuses to admit his mistakes can never
be successful. But if he confesses and forsakes
them, he gets another chance.

The Bible

If you must make mistakes, it will be more to your
credit if you make a new one each time.

He who never made a mistake, never
made a discovery.

Samuel Smiles

If you find a mistake in this paper, please consider
that it was there for a purpose. We publish
something for everyone, including those who
are always looking for mistakes.

Every great mistake has a halfway moment,
a split second when it can be recalled and
perhaps remedied.

Pearl S. Buck

If I had to live my life over again, I'd dare to
make more mistakes next time.

Nadine Stair

MISTRUST

When mistrust enters, love departs.

Mistrust the man who finds everything good, the man
who finds everything evil and, still more the man
who is indifferent to everything.

Lavater

MISUNDERSTANDING

Is it so bad, then, to be misunderstood? Pythagoras
was misunderstood, and Socrates, and Jesus, and
Luther, and Copernicus, and Galileo, and Newton,

and every pure and wise spirit that ever took flesh.
To be great is to be misunderstood.
Emerson

MODESTY

A modest man never talks of himself.
La Bruyere

MONDAY

Monday is a terrible way to spend
one-seventh of your life.
Houghton Line

MONEY

When I have any money I get rid of it as quickly as
possible, lest it find a way into my heart.
John Wesley

The safest way to double your money is to fold it
over once and put it in your pocket.
Frank McKinney Hubbard

That money talks
I'll not deny,
I heard it once:
It said, "Goodbye."
Richard Armour

Money is a terrible master but an excellent servant.
P. T. Barnum

It's peculiar how a dollar can look so big when it goes
to church and so small when it goes for groceries.

To figure your cost of living simply take your income and add 10 percent.

Today women often push carts through at speeds over $65 an hour.

Joseph Salak

If you would know the value of money, go and try to borrow some.

Benjamin Franklin

Just about the time you think you can make both ends meet, somebody moves the ends.

Spend less than you get.

If your outgo exceeds your income, then your upkeep will be your downfall.

When money speaks, the truth is silent.

The love of money is the root of all evil.

The Bible

Money mad. My wife says I spend money like a drunken sailor. Wonder what she'd say if I spent it like a sober congressman?

R. W. Plagge

Money doesn't talk these days—it goes without saying.

A man's treatment of money is the most decisive test of his character—how he makes it and how he spends it.

James Moffatt

Those who believe money can do everything are frequently prepared to do everything for money.

I'd like to live like a poor man—only with lots of money.

Pablo Picasso

Beware of the little expenses;
A small leak will sink a great ship.

Benjamin Franklin

MORALITY

The new morality is terrible. It's taken all the sting out of gossip.

To give a man full knowledge of true morality,
I would send him to no other book than
the New Testament.

Locke

Let us with caution indulge the supposition that morality can be maintained without religion. Reason and experience both forbid us to expect that national morality can prevail in exclusion of religious principle.

George Washington

Right is right, even if everyone is against it; and wrong is wrong, even if everyone is for it.

William Penn

If we ever pass out as a great nation, we ought to put on our tombstone: "America died of the delusion that she had moral leadership."

Will Rogers

We do many things at the federal level that would be considered dishonest and illegal if done in the private sector.

Donald Regan

MORNING

The early morning has gold in its mouth.

Benjamin Franklin

MOTHERS

An ounce of mother is worth more than a pound of clergy.

H. H. Birkins

God could not be everywhere and, therefore he made mothers.

MOTIVATION

Motivation is what gets you started. Habit is what keeps you going.

Jim Ryun

People are always motivated by at least two reasons; the one they tell you about, and a secret one.

O. A. Battista

We can justify our every deed but God looks at our motives.

The Bible

MOUNTAINS

They say they climb mountains because they
are there. I wonder if it would astound them to
know that the very same reason is why
the rest of us go around them.

S. Omar Barker

MOURN

He that lacks time to mourn, lacks time to mend.

Sir Henry Taylor

MURDER

Every unpunished murder takes away something
from the security of every man's life.

Daniel Webster

MUSIC

Music hath charms to soothe the savage beast.

James Bramston

Music hath charm to soothe a savage beast—but I'd
try a revolver first.

Josh Billings

NATURE

Nature is a volume of which God is the author.

Harvey

NECESSITY

Necessity is the mother of invention.

NEIGHBOR

No one is rich enough to do without a neighbor.

When your neighbor's house is afire your
own property is at stake.

Horace

NERVOUS BREAKDOWN

One of the symptoms of an approaching nervous breakdown is the belief that one's work is terribly important.

Bertrand Russell

NEUTRALITY

The hottest places in hell are reserved for those who in time of great moral crises maintain their neutrality.

Dante Alighieri

NEWSPAPER

If newspapers are useful in overthrowing tyrants, it is only to establish a tyranny of their own.

James Fenimore Cooper

I fear three newspapers more than a hundred thousand bayonets.

Napoleon Bonaparte

The old saw says, "Let a sleeping dog lie." Right. Still when there is much at stake it is better to get a newspaper to do it.

NICE

This would be a great world if everyone was as nice to you as the guy who's trying to sell you something.

Be nice to people on your way up because you'll meet them on your way down.

Wilson Mizner

NO

Learn to say no; it will be of more use to you
than to be able to read Latin.

Charles H. Spurgeon

NOAH

Such is the human race. Often it does seem such a
pity that Noah . . . didn't miss the boat.

Mark Twain

NONCONFORMITY

If there is anything the nonconformist hates
worse than a conformist, it's another nonconformist
who doesn't conform to the prevailing standards
of nonconformity.

Bill Vaughan

Comedy is the last refuge of the
nonconformist mind.

Gilbert Seldes

Whenever I draw a circle, I immediately want
to step out of it.

R. Buckminster Fuller

NO PARKING

You can always recognize a no-parking area.
There are fewer cars there.

Franklin P. Jones

NOTHING

The only thing necessary for the triumph of evil
is for good men to do nothing.
Edmund Burke

Originates nothing, anticipates nothing,
takes no responsibility, plans nothing, suggests
nothing, is good for nothing.
Gideon Welles

Sometimes one pays most for the things
one gets for nothing.
Albert Einstein

NOVEL

There are three rules for writing a novel.
Unfortunately, no one knows what they are.
W. Somerset Maugham

Every novel should have a beginning,
a muddle, and an end.
Peter De Vries

The great American novel has not only already been
written, it has already been rejected.
Frank Dane

OBEDIENCE

Every great person has first learned how to obey,
whom to obey, and when to obey.

William Ward

What a scarcity of news there would be if we all
obeyed the Ten Commandments.

OFFEND

It is harder to win back the friendship of an offended
brother than to capture a fortified city. His anger
shuts you out like iron bars.

The Bible

OLD AGE

One cannot help being old, but one
can resist being aged.

Lord Samuel

A man is not old until regrets
take the place of dreams.
John Barrymore

Of late I appear
To have reached that stage
When people look old
Who are only my age.
Richard Armour

You know you're getting old when the candles
cost more than the cake.
Bob Hope

If I'd known I was going to live so long, I'd
have taken better care of myself.
Leon Eldred

Every man desires to live long,
but no man would be old.
Jonathan Swift

To me, old age is always fifteen years
older than I am.
Bernard Baruch

Old age isn't so bad . . . when you consider
the alternative.

In youth the days are short and the years are long; in
old age the years are short and the days long.
Panin

I enjoy my wrinkles and regard them
as badges of distinction—I've
worked hard for them!
Maggie Kuhn

Just remember, once you're over the hill you begin to pick up speed.

Charles Schulz

Take care that old age does not wrinkle your spirit even more than your face.

Michel de Montaigne

As we advance in life, we acquire a keener sense of the value of time. Nothing else, indeed, seems of any consequence; and we become misers in this respect.

William Hazlitt

When saving for old age, be sure to lay up a few pleasant thoughts.

ONE PICTURE IS A THOUSAND WORDS

One picture worth a thousand words? You give me 1,000 words and I can have the Lord's Prayer, the twenty-third psalm, the Hippocratic oath, a sonnet by Shakespeare, the Preamble to the Constitution, Lincoln's Gettysburg address, and I'd have enough left over for just about all of the Boy Scout oath and I wouldn't trade you for any picture on earth.

OPENNESS

Keep an open mind, but don't keep it too open or people will throw a lot of rubbish into it.

If you come at me with your fists doubled, I think I can promise you that mine will double as fast as yours; but if you come to me and say, "Let us sit down and take counsel together, and, if we differ from one another, understand why it is we differ from one another, just what the points at issue are," we will presently find that we are not so far apart after all, that the points on which we differ are few and the points on which we agree are many, and that if we only have the patience and the candor and the desire to get together, we will get together.

Woodrow Wilson

OPINIONS

It is not best that we should all think alike; it is difference of opinion which makes horse races.

Mark Twain

New opinions are always suspected, and usually opposed, without any other reason but because they are not already common.

John Locke

To obtain a man's opinion of you, make him mad.

Oliver Wendell Holmes

The feeble tremble before opinion, the foolish defy it, the wise judge it, the skillful direct it.

Jeanne de la Platiere

A good sleep and some
exercise changes
many opinions.

R. E. Phillips

OPPORTUNITY

Opportunity is missed by most people because
it is dressed in overalls and looks like work.

Thomas Edison

Our ship would come in much sooner if
we'd swim out to meet it.

Opportunities multiply as they are seized;
they die when neglected.

The reason so many people never get anywhere in
life is because, when opportunity knocks, they are
out in the backyard looking for four-leaf clovers.

Walter P. Chrysler

When one door closes, another opens; but we often
look so long and so regretfully upon the closed door
that we do not see the one which has opened for us.

Alexander Graham Bell

Four things come not back—the spoken word,
the sped arrow, the past life, and the
neglected opportunity.

When written in Chinese, the word crisis is composed
of two characters—one represents danger and the
other represents opportunity.

John F. Kennedy

Gentlemen, we're surround by
insurmountable opportunities.

Pogo

I always tried to turn every disaster into
an opportunity.

John D. Rockefeller

Do you see difficulties in every opportunity or
opportunities in every difficulty?

Learn to listen. Opportunity could be knocking at
your door very softly.

Frank Tyger

OPTIMISM

Some people are always grumbling because roses
have thorns; I am thankful that thorns have roses.

Alphonse Karr

An optimist may see a light where there is none, but
why must the pessimist always run to blow it out?

Michel de Saint-Piere

An optimist is a fellow who believes a housefly is
looking for a way to get out.

George Nathan

No man ever injured his eyesight by looking
on the bright side of things.

In the long run, the pessimist may be proved right,
but the optimist has a better time on the trip.

ORATORY

When Demosthenes was asked what were the three most important aspects of oratory, he answered, "Action, Action, Action."

Plutarch

ORIGINALITY

Originality is the art of concealing your source.

Franklin P. Jones

OTHERS

It is when we forget ourselves that we do things that are most likely to be remembered.

Unless life is lived for others, it is not worthwhile.

Mother Teresa

OUTLOOK

If the only tool you have is a hammer, you tend to see every problem as a nail.

Reflect upon your present blessings, of which every man has plenty; not on your past misfortunes, of which all men have some.

Charles Dickens

The world is round and the place which may seem like the end may also be the beginning.

Ivy Baker Priest

PAIN

The real problem is not why some pious, humble, believing people suffer, but why some do not.

C. S. Lewis

Pain is an energy monster; we give it the power to hurt us. And we can take that power away— depending on how we choose to view ourselves. All pain is real, but you can change your reality.

David Black

PARENTHOOD

Parents can give everything but common sense.

Who takes the child by the hand takes the mother by the heart.

To bring up a child in the way he should go, travel that way yourself once in a while.

Josh Billings

Tired mothers find that spanking takes less time than reasoning and penetrates sooner to the seat of the memory.

Will Durant

Train a child in the way he should go, and when he is old he will not depart from it.

The Bible

Most of us become parents long before we have stopped being children.

Mignon McLaughlin

PAST

It's futile to talk too much about the past—something like trying to make birth control retroactive.

Charles E. Wilson

The past is but the beginning of a beginning.

H. G. Wells

The past always looks better than it was; it's only pleasant because it isn't here.

Finley P. Dunne

Never worry about anything that is past. Charge it up to experience and forget the trouble. There are always plenty of troubles ahead, so don't turn and look back on any behind you.

Herbert Hoover

That which is past is gone and irrevocable, and wise men have enough to do with things present and to come; therefore they do but trifle with themselves that labor in past matters.

Francis Bacon

All the king's horses and all the king's men can't put the past together again. So let's remember; don't try to saw sawdust.

Dale Carnegie

Forget the past. No one becomes successful in the past.

PATHETIC

The most pathetic person in the world is someone who has sight, but has no vision.

Helen Keller

PATIENCE

Be patient and you will finally win, for a soft tongue can break hard bones.

The Bible

Prayer of the modern American: "Dear God, I pray for patience. And I want it right now!"

Oren Arnold

An ounce of patience is worth a pound of brains.

Young folks should cultivate patience with old folks so that when they grow old they'll have patience with young folks.

Patience is a most necessary qualification for
business; many a man would rather you heard his
story than granted his request.

Lord Chesterfield

One moment of patience may ward off great disaster;
one moment of impatience may ruin a whole life.

Patience is something you admire in the driver
behind you, but not in the one ahead.

Bill McGlashen

If we would like to develop more patience, we
should prepare for trouble.

R. E. Phillips

Everything comes to him who hustles while he waits.

Thomas A. Edison

PATRIOTISM

I venture to suggest that patriotism is not a short and
frenzied outburst of emotion but the tranquil and
steady dedication of a lifetime.

Adlai Stevenson

Patriotism is easy to understand in America;
it means looking out for yourself by looking out
for your country.

Calvin Coolidge

A man who is good enough to shed his blood
for his country is good enough to be given
a square deal afterwards.

Theodore Roosevelt

PAYMASTER

God is a sure paymaster. He may not pay
at the end of every week, or month, or year, but
remember He pays in the end.

Anne of Austria

PEACE

Peace is the deliberate adjustment of my life
to the will of God.

Have courage for the great sorrows of life and
patience for the small ones; and when you have
laboriously accomplished your daily task, go to sleep
in peace. God is awake.

Victor Hugo

Peace is more important than all justice; and peace
was not made for the sake of justice, but justice
for the sake of peace.

Martin Luther

Making peace is the most difficult work of all.

To be at peace with one's self is a joy unspeakable.

R. E. Phillips

Peace and justice are two sides of the same coin.

Dwight D. Eisenhower

PEN

The pen is mightier than the sword.

Bulwer-Lytton

PEOPLE

Too bad that all the people who know how to run
the country are busy driving taxicabs
and cutting hair.

George Burns

All mankind is divided into three classes: those that
are immovable, those that are movable,
and those that move.

Benjamin Franklin

People who fight fire with fire usually
end up with ashes.

Abigail Van Buren

There are two kinds of people in the world: those
who come into a room and say, "Here I am!" and
those who come in and say, "Ah, there you are!"

PERFECTIONIST

A perfectionist is a man who takes infinite pains
and gives them to others.

Alan Benner

PERSEVERANCE

Every calling is great when greatly pursued.

Oliver Wendell Holmes

Victory belongs to the most persevering.

Napoleon Bonaparte

Perseverance is not a long race; it is many short races one after another.

Walter Elliott

Even the woodpecker owes his success to the fact that he uses his head and keeps pecking away until he finishes the job he starts.

Coleman Cox

Little strokes fell great oaks.

Nothing in the world can take the place of persistence. Talent will not; nothing is more common than unsuccessful men with talent. Genius will not; unrewarded genius is almost a proverb. Education will not; the world is full of educated derelicts. Persistence and determination alone are omnipotent. The slogan "Press on" has solved and always will solve the problems of the human race.

Calvin Coolidge

It has been my observation that most people get ahead during the time that others waste.

PERSPIRATION

Genius is one percent inspiration and ninety-nine percent perspiration.

Thomas A. Edison

PERSUASION

I sit here all day trying to persuade people to do the things they ought to have sense enough to do without my persuading them. That's all the powers of the President amount to.

Harry S. Truman

Few are open to conviction, but the majority of men are open to persuasion.

Johann Wolfgang von Goethe

PESSIMISM

A pessimist is one who feels bad when he feels good for fear he'll feel worse when he feels better.

A pessimist? A man who thinks everybody is as nasty as himself, and hates them for it.

George Bernard Shaw

There is no sadder sight than a young pessimist.

Mark Twain

Pessimist: One who, when he has the choice of two evils, chooses both.

Oscar Wilde

PHILOSOPHY

To be a real philosopher one must be able to laugh at philosophy.

Blaise Pascal

I've developed a new philosophy . . . I only dread one day at a time.

Charlie Brown

PHYSICIAN

Every physician almost hath his favorite disease.

Henry Fielding

I am dying with the help of too many physicians.

Alexander the Great

Whenever he saw three physicians together, he
looked up to discover whether there was not a turkey
buzzard in the neighborhood.

Thomas Jefferson

We may lay it down as a maxim, that when
a nation abounds in physicians
it grows thin of people.

Joseph Addison

PITY

He that hath pity upon the poor lendeth unto the
Lord; and that which he hath given
will he pay him again.

The Bible

PLAGIARISM

When a thing has been said and said well, have no
scruple. Take it and copy it.

Anatole France

Taking something from one man and making
it worse is plagiarism.

George Moore

There is much difference between imitating a man
and counterfeiting him.

Benjamin Franklin

What a good thing Adam had. When he said a good thing, he knew nobody had said it before.

Mark Twain

Originality is undetected plagiarism.

William R. Inge

Genius borrows nobly.

Emerson

Nothing is said which has not been said before.

Terence

PLANS

Don't brag about your plans for tomorrow—wait and see what happens.

The Bible

Our plans miscarry because they have no aim. When a man does not know what harbor he is making for, no wind is the right wind.

Seneca

PLAY

There is less in this (play) than meets the eye.

Tallulah Bankhead

To play is to yield oneself to a kind of magic.

Hugo Rabner

PLEASANTNESS

It is easier to catch flies with honey than
with vinegar.

PLEASURE

There is no pleasure in having nothing to do; the fun
is in having lots to do and not doing it.
Mary Wilson Little

That man is the richest whose pleasures
are the cheapest.
Henry David Thoreau

Most of us miss out on life's big prizes. The Pulitzer.
The Nobel. Oscars. Emmys. But we're all eligible for
life's small pleasures. A pat on the back. A kiss
behind the ear. A four-pound bass. A full moon. An
empty parking space. A crackling fire. A great meal.
A glorious sunset. Don't fret about copping life's
grand awards. Enjoy its tiny delights.
There are plenty for all of us.

POLITENESS

It is wise to apply the refined oil of politeness
to the mechanism
of friendship.
Colette

POLITICS

The Democratic Party is like a mule—without pride of
ancestry or hope of posterity.
Ignatius Donnelly

Few politicians die, and none resign.
Thomas Jefferson

I'm not an old, experienced hand at politics. But I am now seasoned enough to have learned that the hardest thing about any political campaign is how to win without proving that you are unworthy of winning.
Adlai Stevenson

The essential ingredient of politics is timing.
Pierre Elliott Trudeau

Practical politics consists in ignoring facts.
Henry Adams

Congress is so strange. A man gets up to speak and says nothing. Nobody listens, then everybody disagrees.
Boris Marshalov

What counts is not necessarily the size of the dog in the fight—it's the size of the fight in the dog.
Dwight D. Eisenhower

Dirksen's Three Laws of Politics:
1. Get elected.
2. Get re-elected.
3. Don't get mad, get even.

Politics is more dangerous than war, for in war you are only killed once.
Winston Churchill

One-fifth of the people are against everything all the time.
Robert F. Kennedy

You can fool too many of the people
too much of the time.
James Thurber

I claim not to have controlled events, but confess
plainly that events have controlled me.
Abraham Lincoln

An honest politician is one who, when he is
bought, will stay bought.
Simon Cameron

Too bad ninety percent of the politicians give the
other ten percent a bad reputation.
Henry Kissinger

The famous politician was trying to save
both his faces.
John Gunther

Politics is not a bad profession. If you succeed
there are many rewards, if you disgrace
yourself you can always write a book.
Ronald Reagan

A politician is a man who shakes your hand before
election and your confidence afterward.

Politics . . . excites all that is selfish
and ambitious in man.

I wouldn't call him a cheap politician. He's
costing this country a fortune!

In crime, they say take the money and run.
In politics, they say run, then take the money.

Politics is supposed to be the second oldest profession. I have come to realize that it bears a very close resemblance to the first.

Ronald Reagan

We're overlooking one of the biggest sources of natural gas in the country—politicians.

Herb True

POOR

When you help the poor you are lending to the Lord—and he pays wonderful interest on your loan!

The Bible

Poor is not the person who has too little, but the person who craves more.

Seneca

POPULARITY

Avoid popularity; it has many snares and no real benefits.

William Penn

POTENTIAL

Treat people as if they were what they ought to be and to help them to become what they are capable of being.

Johann Wolfgang von Goethe

POVERTY

Poverty is uncomfortable; but nine times out of ten
the best thing that can happen to a young man
is to be tossed overboard and be
compelled to sink or swim.

James A. Garfield

Poverty is not dishonorable in itself, but only
when it comes from idleness, intemperance,
extravagance, and folly.

Plutarch

POWER

Power intoxicates men. When a man is intoxicated by
alcohol he can recover, but when intoxicated by
power; he seldom recovers.

James F. Byrnes

The measure of man is what he does with power.

Pittacus

Power may justly be compared to a great river; while
kept within its bounds it is both beautiful and useful,
but when it overflows its banks, it is then too
impetuous to be stemmed; it bears down all
before it, and brings destruction and desolation
wherever it comes.

Andrew Hamilton

Power tends to corrupt; absolute power
corrupts absolutely.

Lord Acton

Patience and gentleness is power.
Leigh Hunt

Character is power.
Booker T. Washington

Being powerful is like being a lady. If you
have to tell people you are, you aren't.
Margaret Thatcher

PRAISE

Don't praise yourself; let others do it!
The Bible

The purity of silver and gold can be tested
in a crucible, but a man is tested
by his reaction to men's praise.
The Bible

A bit of fragrance always clings to the
hand that gives you roses.

One thing scientists have discovered is that
often-praised children become more intelligent than
often-blamed ones. If some of your employees are a
bit dumb, perhaps your treatment of them is to
blame. There's a creative element in praise.
Thomas Dreier

He who gets someone else to blow his horn will
find that the sound travels twice as far.

Praise, like gold and diamonds, owes its
value to its scarcity.

PRAYER

We should not permit prayer to be
taken out of the schools; that's the only way
most of us got through.

Sam Levenson

I have been driven many times to my knees by the
overwhelming conviction that I had nowhere else to
go. My own wisdom, and that of all about me
seemed insufficient for the day.

Abraham Lincoln

Prayer does not change God,
but changes him who prays.

Soren Kierkegaard

PREJUDICE

Opinions founded on prejudice are always sustained
with the greatest violence.

Francis Jeffery

Prejudice is the ink with which all history is written.

Mark Twain

He hears but half who hears one party only.

Aeschylus

PRESERVATIVES

I want nothing to do with natural foods. At my age
I need all the preservatives I can get.

George Burns

PRESIDENT

No man will ever bring out of the presidency the
reputation which carries him into it.
Thomas Jefferson

My movements to the chair of government will be
accompanied by feelings not unlike those
of a culprit who is going to the place
of his execution.
George Washington

Seriously, I do not think I am fit for the presidency.
Abraham Lincoln

The four most miserable years of my life . . .
John Adams

Within the first few months I discovered that being
a president is like riding a tiger. A man has to
keep riding or be swallowed.
Harry S. Truman

When I was a boy I was told that anyone
could be president. I'm beginning
to believe it.
Clarence Darrow

From 40 to 60 percent of the presidential office is not
in administration but in morals, politics, and spiritual
leadership. . . . As President of the United States and
servant of God, he has much more to do than to run
a desk at the head of the greatest corporation in the
world. He has to guide a people in the greatest
adventure ever undertaken on the planet.
William Allen White

PRESSURE

He who rides a tiger is afraid to dismount.

The pressure of public opinion is like the pressure of
the atmosphere; you can't see it—but, all the same, it
is sixteen pounds to the square inch.
James Russell Lowell

A diamond is a chunk of coal that made
good under pressure.

PRETENDING

The only good in pretending is the fun we get out of
fooling ourselves that we fool somebody.
Booth Tarkington

PRIDE

Pride is the only disease known to man that makes
everyone sick except the one who has it.
Buddy Robinson

Pride goes before destruction and
haughtiness before a fall.
The Bible

When a man is wrapped up in himself, he
makes a pretty small package.
John Ruskin

Lord . . . where we are wrong, make us
willing to change, and where we are right,
make us easy to live with.
Peter Marshall

He who pats himself on the back
may dislocate his shoulder.

PRINCIPLES

Prosperity is the best protector of principle.

Mark Twain

When a fellow says it ain't the money
but the principle of the thing,
it's the money.

Kin Hubbard

Important principles may and must be flexible.

Abraham Lincoln

It is easier to fight for one's principles
than to live up to them.

Alfred Adler

PROBLEM

If you keep your head when all about
you are losing theirs—you don't
understand the problem.

A problem well stated is a problem half solved.

One of the tests of leadership is the ability to
recognize a problem before it
becomes an emergency.

Arnold H. Glasow

If you can't state your problem in ten words
or less—you don't understand it yourself.

R. G. Campbell

What a pity human beings can't exchange
problems. Everyone knows exactly how
to solve the other fellow's.

Olin Miller

Most people spend more time and energy
going around problems than in trying
to solve them.

Henry Ford

Every problem contains within itself the seeds
of its own solution.

Charles Kettering, the inventor, had a unique method
of solving problems. He would break down each
problem into the smallest possible sub-problems.
Then he did research to find out which sub-problems
had already been solved. He often found that what
looked like a huge problem had previously been
98 percent solved by another. Then he
tackled what was left.

The best way to forget your own problems is to help
someone else solve his.

Problems are only opportunities in work clothes.

Henry J. Kaiser

PROCRASTINATION

If you want to make an easy job seem mighty
hard, just keep putting off doing it.

Olin Miller

Procrastination is my sin.
It brings me naught but sorrow.
I know that I should stop it.
In fact, I will—tomorrow!

Gloria Pitzer

PROMISE

When a man repeats a promise again
and again, he means to fail you.

He who is the most slow in making a promise is the
most faithful in the performance of it.

Rousseau

One who doesn't give the gift he promised is
like a cloud blowing over a desert
without dropping any rain.

The Bible

If you will promise less and do more,
your boss will eventually put your
name on a door.

PROMPTNESS

I am a believer in punctuality though it
makes me very lonely.

E. V. Verrall

PROPAGANDA

The great masses of the people will more easily fall
victims to a big lie than to a small one.

Adolf Hitler

PROPERTY

Property is the fruit of labor: property is desirable;
it is a positive good.

Abraham Lincoln

Thieves respect property. They merely wish the
property to become their property that they may
more perfectly respect it.

G. K. Chesterton

PROPHECY

I always avoid prophesying beforehand, because
it is much better policy to prophesy after the event
has already taken place.

Winston Churchill

PROSPERITY

I'll say this for adversity: People seem to be able to
stand it, and that's more than I can say for prosperity.

Few of us can stand prosperity—
another man's, I mean.

Mark Twain

PROSTITUTE

O my son, trust my advice—stay away from prosti-
tutes. For a prostitute is a deep and narrow grave.
Like a robber, she waits for her victims as one after
another become unfaithful to their wives.

The Bible

PROVERBS

Proverbs are short sentences drawn from
long experiences.

Cervantes

A country can be judged by the quality
of its proverbs.

PSYCHIATRIST

A neurotic is a man who builds a castle in the air.
A psychotic is the man who lives in it. A psychiatrist
is the man who collects the rent.

Jerome Lawrence

Anybody who goes to see a psychiatrist ought
to have his head examined.

Samuel Goldwyn

A psychiatrist is a fellow who asks you a lot of
expensive questions your wife asks for nothing.

Joey Adams

PUN

Hanging is too good for a man who makes puns;
he should be drawn and quoted.

Fred Allen

A pun is the lowest form of humor—when
you don't think of it first.

Oscar Levant

A pun is a pistol let off at the ear; not a feather
to tickle the intellect.

Charles Lamb

PUNCTUAL

The trouble with being punctual is that
nobody's there to appreciate it.

Franklin P. Jones

There is at least one good thing you can
say about punctuality—it is a sure
way to help you enjoy a few minutes
of complete privacy.

O. A. Battista

QUARRELS

One of the little-mentioned but considerable
advantages of rural living is that family quarrels
can't be overheard.

Sydney Harris

It is hard to stop a quarrel once it starts,
so don't let it begin.

The Bible

A quarrel is quickly settled when deserted by one
party; there is no battle unless there be two.

Seneca

The fiercest quarrels do not always argue the
greatest offenses.

Terence

Those who in quarrels interpose
Must often wipe a bloody nose.

John Gay

QUESTIONS

It is better to ask some of the questions than
to know all of the answers.

James Thurber

Ask a dumb question and be embarrassed
for a moment; don't ask it and be
embarrassed for a lifetime.

Better ask twice than lose your way once.

My greatest strength as a consultant is to be ignorant
and ask a few questions.

Peter Drucker

Don't be afraid to ask dumb questions. They're more
easily handled than dumb mistakes.

William Wister Haines

QUOTATION

I often quote myself. It adds spice
to my conversation.

George Bernard Shaw

Next to being witty yourself, the best thing is
being able to quote another's wit.

Christian N. Bovee

I quote others only the better to express myself.

Michel de Montaigne

By necessity, by proclivity, and by delight,
we all quote.

Emerson

The wisdom of the wise and the experience of the
ages are perpetuated by quotations.

Benjamin Disraeli

He who never quotes is never quoted.

Charles H. Spurgeon

RAGE

Folks who fly into a rage always make a bad landing.

RAINBOW

The way I see it, if you want the rainbow, you
gotta put up with the rain.

Dolly Parton

READING

I divide all readers into two classes; those who read
to remember and those who read to forget.

William Lyon Phelps

When we read too fast or too slowly,
we understand nothing.

Blaise Pascal

He who doesn't read good books has no
advantage over the person who
cannot read them.

REBELLION

Rebellion: The words and acts of violence by
people who have been deeply hurt.

R. E. Phillips

A youngster's heart is filled with rebellion, but
punishment will drive it out of him.

The Bible

RECOLLECTION

Take notes on the spot, a note is worth a
cart-load of recollections.

Waldo Emerson

RECONCILIATION

It is much safer to reconcile an enemy than to
conquer him; victory may deprive him of his poison,
but reconciliation of his will.

Feltham

RECREATION

People who cannot find time for recreation are
obliged sooner or later to find time for illness.

John Wanamaker

REGRET

Regret is an appalling waste of energy;
you can't build on it; it's only good for
wallowing in.

Katherine Mansfield

And now, among the fading embers, these in the
main are my regrets: When I am right, no one
remembers; when I am wrong, no one forgets.

REJOICE

Be still, sad heart, and cease repining,
Behind the clouds the sun is shining;
Thy fate is the common fate of all;
Into each life some rain must fall,
Some days must be dark and dreary.

Henry Wadsworth Longfellow

Why is it that we rejoice at a birth and
grieve at a funeral? It is because we are not
the person concerned?

Mark Twain

Rejoice with them that do rejoice, and weep
with them that weep.

The Bible

RELATIONSHIPS

Beware of the danger signals that flag problems:
silence, secretiveness, or sudden outburst.

Sylvia Porter

RELATIVITY

When a man sits with a pretty girl for an hour, it seems like a minute. But let him sit on a hot stove for a minute, and it's longer than an hour. That's relativity.

Albert Einstein

RELAXATION

Only when a man is at peace with himself can he find the inclination to relax.

The time to relax is when you don't have time for it.

Sydney J. Harris

RELIGION

If men are so wicked with religion, what would they be without it?

Benjamin Franklin

Men will wrangle for religion; write for it; fight for it; die for it; anything but—live for it.

Colton

REPENTANCE

It is much easier to repent of sins that we have committed than to repent of those we intend to commit.

Josh Billings

Repentance ain't confined to doing wrong,
sometimes you catch it just as sharp for doing right.
Repentance is not so much remorse for what we
have done as the fear of consequences.

Francois de La Rochefoucauld

REPETITION

Repetition is the mother to talent.

REPRESSION

We have to condemn publicly the very idea that
some people have the right to repress others. In
keeping silent about evil, in burying it so deep within
us that no sign of it appears on the surface, we are
implanting it, and it will rise up a thousandfold in the
future. When we neither punish nor reproach
evildoers . . . we are ripping the foundations
of justice from beneath new generations.

Alexander I. Solzhenitsyn

REPUBLICS

Republics are brought to their ends by luxury;
monarchies by poverty.

Montesquieu

REPUTATION

A reputation may be repaired, but people always
keep their eyes on the place where the crack was.

If you must choose, take a good name rather
than great riches; for to be held in loving
esteem is better than
silver and gold.

The Bible

Judge a man by the reputation of his enemies.

Nothing deflates so fast as a punctured reputation.

Thomas Dewar

Associate yourself with men of good quality if you
esteem your own reputation; for 'tis better to be alone
than in bad company.

George Washington

One man lies in his words and gets a bad reputation;
another in his manners, and enjoys a good one.

Henry David Thoreau

Glass, China, and Reputation are easily crack'd
and never well mended.

Benjamin Franklin

RESOLUTION

Perhaps there is no more important component of
character than steadfast resolution. The boy who is
going to make a great man, or is going to count in
any way in afterlife, must make up his mind not
merely to overcome a thousand obstacles, but to
win in spite of a thousand repulses and defeats.

Theodore Roosevelt

RESOURCEFULNESS

Resourcefulness is the ability to call upon
creativity when needed.

RESPONSIBILITY

For God is closely watching you, and He
weighs carefully everything you do.

Few things help an individual more than to
place responsibility upon him, and to let him
know that you trust him.

Booker T. Washington

You can't escape the responsibility of
tomorrow by evading it today.

Abraham Lincoln

Here is my final conclusion: Fear God and obey his
commandments, for this is the entire duty of man.
For God will judge us for everything we do, including
every hidden thing, good or bad.

The Bible

When your shoulders are carrying a load of
responsibility, there isn't
room for chips.

REST

A light supper, a good night's sleep, and a fine
morning have often made a hero of the same man,
who, by indigestion, a restless night, and a rainy
morning would have proved a coward.

Lord Chesterfield

Take rest; a field that has rested gives
a bountiful crop.

Ovid

Come unto me, all ye that labor and
are heavy laden, and
I will give you rest.

The Bible

RESULTS

The world is not interested in the storms you
encountered, but whether you brought in the ship.

The world expects results. Don't tell others
about the labor pains—show 'em the baby!

Arnold H. Glasow

RETIREMENT

Before deciding to retire, stay home for a week
and watch the daytime TV shows.

Bill Copeland

Retired is being tired twice, I've thought,
first tired of working, then tired of not.

Richard Armour

The fellow who can't figure out what to do with a
Sunday afternoon is often the same one who can't
wait for retirement.

The worst thing about retirement is to have to drink
coffee on your own time.

When some fellers decide to retire, nobody
knows the difference.

Kin Hubbard

The best time to start thinking about your
retirement is before the boss does.

REVENGE

Revenge is often like biting a dog because
the dog bit you.

Austin O'Malley

In taking revenge a man is but equal to his enemy,
but in passing over he is his superior.

Francis Bacon

Vengeance is mine; I will repay, saith the Lord.
Therefore if thine enemy hunger, feed him; if he thirst,
give him drink: for in so doing thou shalt heap coals
of fire on his head.

The Bible

REVERENCE

He that will have his son have a respect for him
and his orders, must himself have a great
reverence for his son.

John Locke

RICH

Trying to get rich quick is evil and leads to poverty.

The Bible

The suffering of the rich is among the sweetest pleasures of the poor.

R. M. Huber

I've been rich and I've been poor; rich is better.

Sophie Tucker

Don't knock the rich. When was the last time you were hired by somebody poor?

Robert Orben

Life begets life. Energy creates energy. It is by spending oneself that one becomes rich.

Sarah Bernhardt

RICHES

A little house well filled, a little land well tilled, and a little wife well willed, are great riches.

The best way to realize the pleasure of feeling rich is to live in a smaller house than your means would entitle you to have.

Edward Clarke

Be rich to yourself and poor to your friends.

Juvenal

RIGHT

My specialty is being right when other people are wrong.

George Bernard Shaw

Right is right, even if everyone is against it; and
wrong is wrong, even if everyone is for it.

William Penn

Always do right. This will gratify some
people and astonish the rest.

Mark Twain

Two wrongs can never make a right.

RIGHTEOUS INDIGNATION

Righteous indignation: your own wrath as opposed
to the shocking bad temper of others.

Elbert Hubbard

RIGHTEOUSNESS

You can always tell when you are on the road
of righteousness—it's uphill.

Ernest Blevins

Some folks in this world spend their whole time
hunting after righteousness and can't find any
time to practice it.

Josh Billings

Righteousness exalteth a nation.

The Bible

RIGHTS

If some people got their rights they would complain
of being deprived of their wrongs.

Oliver Herford

Never yield your courage—your courage
to live, your courage to fight, to resist, to develop
your own lives, to be free. I'm talking about
resistance to wrong and
fighting oppression.

Roger Baldwin

I believe that every right implies a responsibility;
every opportunity, an obligation; every
possession, a duty.

John D. Rockefeller, Jr.

RISK

You can't expect to hit the jackpot if you don't put a
few nickels in the machine.

Flip Wilson

Risk! Risk anything! Care no more for
the opinion of others, for those voices. Do the
hardest thing on earth for you. Act for yourself.
Face the truth.

Katherine Mansfield

Take calculated risks. That is quite different
from being rash.

George S. Patton

RUMOR

Rumor is a pipe blown by surmises,
jealousies, conjectures.

William Shakespeare

Trying to squash a rumor is like
trying to unring a bell.
Shana Alexander

RUT

Some folks will stumble through life getting out
of one rut only to fall into another.

The only difference between a rut and a
grave is their dimensions.
Ellen Glasgow

He who thinks he's in the groove
is often in a rut.

SADNESS

Believe me, every heart has its secret
sorrows, which the world knows not;
and of times we call a man
cold when he is only sad.
Henry Wadsworth Longfellow

SAFETY

The desire for safety stands against every great
and noble enterprise.
Tacitus

The best safety lies in fear.
William Shakespeare

It is better to be safe than sorry.

SARCASM

Sarcasm is jealousy in bold disguise.

Sarcasm comes from the Greek word *sarkasmos*,
which means to rip flesh like dogs or
to gnash the teeth in rage.

R. E. Phillips

SATIRE

The finest satire is that in which ridicule is combined
with so little malice and so much conviction that it
even rouses laughter in those who are hit.

George Christoph Lichtenberg

Satire will always be unpleasant to those
that deserve it.

Thomas Shadwell

SATISFACTION

Unless each day can be looked back upon by an
individual as one in which he has had some fun,
some joy, some real satisfaction, that day is a loss. It
is un-Christian and wicked, in my opinion, to allow
such a thing to occur.

Dwight D. Eisenhower

There is no satisfaction in hanging a man who
does not object to it.

George Bernard Shaw

SCARE

A good scare is worth more to a man
than good advice.

Watson Edger Howe

SCHOOL

If I ran a school, I'd give the average grade to the ones who gave me all the right answers, for being good parrots. I'd give the top grades to those who made a lot of mistakes and told me about them, and then told me what they learned from them.

R. Buckminster Fuller

I have never let my schooling interfere with my education.

Mark Twain

Describing her first day back in grade school, after a long absence, a teacher said, "It was like trying to hold 35 corks under water at the same time."

Mark Twain

SCIENCE

Many scientists have quit wondering how old the earth is and have begun pondering how much older it will get.

I shall make electricity so cheap that only the rich can afford to burn candles.

Thomas A. Edison

It is inexcusable for scientists to torture animals; let them make their experiments on journalists and politicians.

Henrik Ibsen

★273★

Law of Hydrodynamics: When the body is immersed in water, the telephone rings.

SECRET

If you would keep your secret from an enemy, tell it not to a friend.

Benjamin Franklin

He who tells a secret is another man's servant.

Three may keep a secret if two of them are dead.

Benjamin Franklin

SECRETARY

Starting as a secretary is a shrewd course for any ambitious young woman. It plugs you in at a higher level than most entry-level jobs. You can eavesdrop and learn a lot.

Joan Manley

SECURITY

Security is mortal's chiefest enemy.

Ellen Terry

Life is certainly only worthwhile as it represents struggle for worthy causes. There is no struggle in perfect security. I am quite certain that the human being could not continue to exist if he had perfect security.

Dwight D. Eisenhower

If all that Americans want is security, then they can go to prison. They'll have enough to eat, a bed, and a roof over their heads.

Dwight D. Eisenhower

Life is either a daring adventure or nothing at all. Security is mostly a superstition. It does not exist in nature.

Helen Keller

SELF-CONFIDENCE

Self-confidence is the first requisite to great undertakings.

Samuel Johnson

SELF-CONTROL

It is better to be slow-tempered than famous; it is better to have self-control than to control an army.

The Bible

He is the greatest conqueror who has conquered himself.

Nothing gives one person so much advantage over another as to remain always cool and unruffled under all circumstances.

Thomas Jefferson

Educate your children to self-control, to the habit of holding passion and prejudice and evil tendencies subject to an upright and reasoning will,

and you have done much to abolish misery
from their future lives and crimes from society.
Daniel Webster

If you begin by denying yourself nothing, the world
later is apt to do your denying for you.
B. F. Forbes

SELF-DISCIPLINE

What we do upon some great occasion will probably
depend on what we already are; and what we are
will be the result of previous years of self-discipline.
H. P. Liddon

To be able to dispense with good things is
tantamount to possessing them.
Jean Francois Regnard

SELF-PITY

Sometimes I get the feeling that the whole world is
against me—but deep down I know that's not true.
Some of the smaller countries are neutral.
Robert Orben

SELF-RESPECT

Self-respect is the compensation you receive for
respecting the rights of others.

The willingness to accept responsibility for
one's own life is the source from which
self-respect springs.
Joan Didion

SELF-SUFFICIENT

No man is an island, entire of itself; every man is a piece of the continent, a part of the main.

John Donne

SELFISHNESS

He who lives to benefit himself confers on the world a benefit when he dies.

Tertullian

He that falls in love with himself will have no rivals.

Benjamin Franklin

SENATE

If we in the Senate would stop calling each other "distinguished," we might have ten working days a year.

Edward W. Brooke

If you're hanging around with nothing to do and the zoo is closed, come over to the Senate. You'll get the same kind of feeling and you won't have to pay.

Robert Dole

Never blame a legislative body for not doing something. When they do nothing, they don't hurt anybody. When they do something is when they become dangerous.

Will Rogers

SERVICE

When people are serving, life is no
longer meaningless.

John Gardner

It is high time that the ideal of success should be
replaced by the ideal of service.

Albert Einstein

If the world is cold, make it your
business to build fires.

Horace Traubel

If you wish to be a leader you will be frustrated, for
very few people wish to be led. If you aim to be a
servant you will never be frustrated.

Frank F. Warren

God is not greater if you reverence Him, but you are
greater if you serve Him.

Augustine

He who serves well need not fear to ask his wages.

SICKNESS

Sickness has four stages: ill, pill, bill, will.

SILENCE

Silence is one of the hardest things to refute.

Josh Billings

Silence is the wisest of replies.

R. E. Phillips

There are three times when you should never
say anything important to a person: when he is
tired, when he is angry, and when he has just
made a mistake.

A man is known by the silence he keeps.

Oliver Herford

Silence, along with modesty, is a great
aid to conversation.

Michel de Montaigne

Silence. All human unhappiness comes from not
knowing how to stay quietly in a room.

Blaise Pascal

Sticks and stones are hard on bones
Aimed with angry art,
Words can sting like anything
But silence breaks the heart.

Phyllis McGinley

SIMPLIFY

The ability to simplify means to eliminate the
unnecessary so that the necessary may speak.

Hans Hoffman

SIN

All my life I have been seeking to climb out
of the pit of my besetting sins and I cannot

do it and I never will unless a hand is
let down to draw me up.

Seneca

The instances are exceedingly rare of men
immediately passing over a clear marked line from
virtue into declared vice and corruption. There are
middle tints and shades between the two extremes;
there is something uncertain on the confines of the
two empires which they must pass through, and
which renders the change easy and imperceptible.

Edmund Burke

There is no sin without previous preparation.

SINCERITY

Sincerity is an openness of heart; we find it
in very few people.

Francois de La Rochefoucauld

I should say sincerity, a deep, great genuine
sincerity, is the characteristic of all men
in any way heroic.

Thomas Carlyle

SITUATIONS

It is not the situation that makes the man, but the man
who makes the situation. The slave may be a
freeman. The monarch may be a slave. Situations
are noble or ignoble, as we make them.

Frederick W. Robertson

SKEPTICISM

Skepticism is a hedge against vulnerability.
Charles Thomas Samuels

Never trust a man who speaks well of everybody.
John Churton Collins

SLANDER

A slander is like a hornet; if you cannot kill it dead the
first blow, better not strike at it.
H. W. Shaw

SLAVERY

Whenever I hear anyone arguing for slavery,
I feel a strong impulse to see it
tried on him personally.
Abraham Lincoln

SLEEP

The vigorous are no better than the lazy during one
half of life, for all men are alike when asleep.
Aristotle

Sleep is the best cure for waking troubles.
Cervantes

SMILE

A smile costs nothing but gives much. It enriches
those who receive without making poorer those who
give. It takes but a moment, but the memory of it

sometimes lasts forever. None is so rich or mighty that he can get along without it and none is so poor that he cannot be made rich by it. A smile creates happiness in the home, fosters goodwill in business, and is the countersign of friendship. It brings rest to the weary, cheer to the discouraged, sunshine to the sad, and is nature's best antidote for trouble. Yet it cannot be bought, begged, borrowed, or stolen, for it is something that is of no value to anyone until it is given away. Some people are too tired to give you a smile. Give them one of yours, as none needs a smile so much as he who has no more to give.

Smile at people. It takes seventy-two muscles to frown, only fourteen to smile.

The most powerful single thing you can do to have influence over others is to smile at them.

Most smiles are started by another smile.

Frank A. Clark

SMOKING

To cease smoking is the easiest thing I ever did; I ought to know because I've done it a thousand times.

Mark Twain

Much smoking kills live men and cures dead swine.

Smoking won't send you to hell. It will just make you smell like you've been there.

R. E. Phillips

SNORE

People who snore always fall asleep first.

SOBRIETY

Water, taken in moderation, cannot hurt anybody.
Mark Twain

SOCIALISM

The function of socialism is to
raise suffering to a higher level.
Norman Mailer

There are two places only where socialism
will work; in heaven where it is not needed, and
in hell where they already have it.
Winston Churchill

SOLITUDE

Solitude: A good place to visit, but a
poor place to stay.
Josh Billings

The best thinking has been done in solitude. The
worst has been done in turmoil.
Thomas A. Edison

SORROW

There is a sweet joy which
comes to us through sorrow.
Charles H. Spurgeon

Every heart hath its own ache.
Thomas Fuller

Sorrow is like a precious treasure,
shown only to friends.

Never allow your own sorrow to absorb you,
but seek out another to console, and you
will find consolation.
J. C. Macaulay

There can be no rainbow
without a cloud and a storm.
J. H. Vincent

People who drink to drown their sorrow
should be told that sorrow
knows how to swim.
Ann Landers

Don't look at the ground when you say, "I'm sorry."
Hold your head up and look the person in the eye,
so he'll know you mean it.
Susan Jacoby

SPEAK

Do you wish men to speak well of you? Then
never speak well of yourself.
Blaise Pascal

First learn the meaning of what you say,
and then speak.

Epictetus

I served with General Washington in the Legislature of
Virginia . . . and . . . with Doctor Franklin in Congress.
I never heard either of them speak ten minutes at a
time, nor to any but the main point.

Thomas Jefferson

I like people who refuse to speak until they
are ready to speak.

SPEAKING

If you haven't struck oil in your first three
minutes, stop boring!

George Jessel

SPECULATE

There are two times in a man's life when he
should not speculate: when he can't afford it,
and when he can.

Mark Twain

SPEECH

More have repented of speech than silence.

Three things matter in a speech: who says it, how he
says it, and what he says . . . and, of the three, the
last matters the least.

Lord Morley

The more you say, the less people remember.

Anatole France

The difference between a successful career and a
mediocre one sometimes consists of leaving about

four or five things a day unsaid.
It usually takes me more than three weeks to
prepare a good impromptu speech.

Mark Twain

I disapprove of what you say, but I will
defend to the death your right to say it.

Voltaire

SPIRIT

Spirit . . . has fifty times the strength and
staying-power of brawn and muscle.

SPORT

The trouble with being a good sport is that
you have to lose to prove it.

Sports like baseball, football, basketball, and hockey
develop muscles. That's why Americans have the
strongest eyes in the world.

Robert Orben

Sports do not build character. They reveal it.

Haywood Broun

STEALING

He who steals a pin will steal a greater thing.

In vain we call old notions fudge,
And bend our conscience to our dealing;
The Ten Commandments will not budge,
And stealing will continue stealing.

James Russell Lowell

STOCK MARKET

They call him a broker because, after you
see him, you are.

When I saw how badly my shares were doing, I
tried to call my broker—but his ledge was busy.

If stock market experts were so expert, they
would be buying stock, not selling advice.

Norman Augustine

STRENGTH

One, on God's side, is a majority.

Wendell Phillips

My strength is made perfect in weakness.

The Bible

Few men during their lifetime come anywhere near
exhausting the resources dwelling within them.
There are deep wells
of strength that are never used.

Richard E. Byrd

I've never been one who thought the Lord
should make life easy; I've just asked Him
to make me strong.

Eva Bowring

STRIFE

It is an honor for a man to stay out of a fight.
Only fools insist on quarreling.

The Bible

STRUGGLE

The important thing in life is not the triumph
but the struggle.

Pierre de Coubertin

We are not at our best perched at the summit;
we are climbers, at our best when the way is steep.

John W. Gardner

STUPIDITY

He was born stupid and greatly
improved his birthright.

Samuel Butler

Ordinarily he is insane. But he has lucid
moments when he is only stupid.

Heinrich Heine

SUBTLETY

Subtlety is the art of saying what you think and
getting out of range before it is understood.

SUCCESS

Success is the one unpardonable sin
against one's fellows.

Ambrose Bierce

Success has made failures of many men.

Success is simply a matter of luck.
Ask any failure.
Earl Wilson

Eighty percent of success is showing up.
Woody Allen

Success consists of getting up just one
more time than you fall.
Oliver Goldsmith

If you want to know how long it will take to get to the
top, consult a calendar. If you want to know how
long it takes to fall to the bottom, try a stopwatch.

It takes about twenty years to become
an overnight success.
Eddie Cantor

Success covers a multitude of blunders.
George Bernard Shaw

This is the foundation of success nine times out of
ten—having confidence in yourself and applying
yourself with all your might to your work.
Thomas A. Wilson

I can give you a six-word formula for success:
"Think things through—then follow through."
Edward Vernon Rickenbacker

That man is a success who has lived well, laughed
often, and loved much; who has gained the respect
of intelligent men and the love of children; who has
filled his niche and accomplished his task; who
leaves the world better than he found it, whether by
an improved poppy, a perfect poem, or a rescued

soul; who never lacked appreciation of earth's beauty
or failed to express it; who looked for the best
in others and gave the best he had.

Robert Louis Stevenson

The toughest thing about success is that you've got
to keep on being a success.

Irving Berlin

SUFFERING

Out of suffering have emerged the strongest souls;
the most massive characters are sheared with scars.

E. H. Chapin

You must submit to supreme suffering in
order to discover the completion of joy.

John Calvin

No pain, no palm; no thorns, no throne; no gall, no
glory; no cross, no crown.

William Penn

No pain, no gain.

Tragedy is in the eye of the observer, and
not in the heart of the sufferer.

Ralph Waldo Emerson

The truth that many people never understand, until it
is too late, is that the more you try to avoid suffering
the more you suffer because smaller and more
insignificant things begin to torture you in proportion
to your fear of being hurt.

Thomas Merton

Although the world is full of suffering, it is full
also of the overcoming of it.
Helen Keller

SUNRISE

If God wanted us to enjoy sunrises, He
would have made them come at
10:00 in the morning.
Jim Slevcove

SUNSHINE

Those who bring sunshine into the lives of
others cannot keep it from themselves.
James M. Barrie

SWEARING

Profane swearing never did any man any good. No
man is the richer or wiser or happier for it.
Louth

SYMPATHY

No one really understands the grief or
joy of another.
Franz Schubert

In all matters of opinion, our
adversaries are insane.
Mark Twain

TACT

Tact: Ability to tell a man he's open-minded when he has a hole in his head.

F. G. Kernan

Do not use a hatchet to remove a fly from your friend's forehead.

Tact is the ability to describe others as they see themselves.

Abraham Lincoln

Tact is the art of making a point without making an enemy.

The nearer you come in relation with a person, the more necessary do tact and courtesy become.

Oliver Wendell Holmes

TALENT

There is no such thing as talent.
There is pressure.
Alfred Adler

TALK

Don't talk so much. You keep putting your foot in
your mouth. Be sensible and turn off the flow!
The Bible

After all is said and done, more is said than done.

Don't be afraid to talk to yourself. It's the only way
you can be sure somebody's listening.
Franklin P. Jones

It is all right if you talk to yourself. It is all right if
you answer yourself. But when you start disagreeing
with the answers, you've got a problem.
R. E. Phillips

Talk to a man about himself and he will
listen for hours.
Benjamin Disraeli

Great boaster, little doer.

Better to let them wonder why you didn't talk than
why you did.

The secret of being tiresome is in telling everything.
Voltaire

If you have something to do that is worthwhile, don't talk about it—do it. After you've done it your friends will talk about it.

TAX COLLECTOR

What is the difference between a taxidermist and a tax collector? The taxidermist takes only your skin.

Mark Twain

The tax collector must love poor people—he's creating so many of them.

Bill Vaughan

TAXES

The Eiffel Tower is the Empire State Building after taxes.

Next to being shot at and missed, nothing is quite as satisfying as an income tax refund.

F. J. Raymond

Render therefore unto Caesar the things which are Caesar's; and unto God the things that are God's.

The Bible

Death and taxes may be the only certainties in life, but nowhere is it written that we have to tax ourselves to death.

It seems a little ridiculous now, but this country was originally founded as a protest against taxation.

Taxation without representation is tyranny.

James Otis

Taxation with representation ain't so hot either.

Gerald Barzan

No matter how bad a child is, he is still good
for a tax deduction.

Milk the cow but do not pull off the udder.

I'm proud to be paying taxes in the United States.
The only thing is, I could be just as proud for
half the money.

Arthur Godfrey

The income tax has made more liars out of
American people than golf has.

Will Rogers

It has reached a point where taxes are a form
of capital punishment.

A taxpayer is someone who works for the federal
government but who doesn't have to take a
civil service examination.

Ronald Reagan

All the money nowadays seems to be produced
with a natural homing instinct for the IRS.

R. E. Phillips

I'm putting all my money in taxes—it is the
only thing sure to go up.

The hardest thing in the world to understand
is the income tax.

Albert Einstein

Even Albert Einstein reportedly needed
help on his 1040 form.

Ronald Reagan

I hold in my hand 1,379 pages of
tax simplification.

Delbert Latta

TEACH

To teach is to learn twice.

Joseph Joubert

One man may teach another to speak,
but none can teach another to hold his peace.

To teach a man how he may learn to grow
independently, and for himself, is perhaps the
greatest service that one man can do to another.

Benjamin Jowett

TEACHER

A teacher affects eternity; no one can tell where
his influence stops.

Henry Adams

I had, out of my sixty teachers, a scant half dozen
who couldn't have been supplanted by phonographs.

Don Herold

To teach is to learn.

I hear and I forget. I see and I remember.
I do and I understand.

TEAM SPIRIT

If anything goes bad, I did it.
If anything goes semi-good, then we did it.
If anything goes real good, then you did it.
Bear Bryant

TEARS

More tears are shed in our theaters over fancied
tragedies than in our churches over real ones.
Frank C. Rideout

TEENAGER

Nobody can be so amusingly arrogant as
a young man who has just discovered an old idea
and thinks it is his own.
Sydney Harris

Sometimes a young person is bad because
he hates to waste a reputation.
John K. Young

There's nothing wrong with teenagers that
reasoning with them won't aggravate.

To get his teenage son to clean his room one
father just throws the keys to the family car
in there once a week.
Lane Olinghouse

It is amazing how quickly the kids learn to drive a car, yet are unable to understand the lawnmower, snowblower, or vacuum cleaner.

Ben Bergor

Remember that as a teenager you are in the last stage of your life when you will be happy to hear the phone is for you.

Fran Liebowitz

It's foolish to worry about confused, miserable teenagers. Give them a few years and they'll turn out to be normal, miserable adults.

TELEVISION

Television has changed the American child from an irresistible force into an immovable object.

Television requires nothing of us, but in requiring nothing, takes the most valuable possession we have: our time.

I find television very educating. Every time somebody turns on the set I go into the other room and read a book.

Groucho Marx

Pure drivel tends to drive ordinary drivel off the TV screen.

Marvin Kitman

The easiest way to find more time to do all the things you want to do is to turn off the television.

O. A. Battista

TV has come a long way. First it was black and white. Then it was color. Now it's off-color.

TEMPER

When you are right you can afford to keep your temper; when you are wrong, you can't afford to lose it.

TEMPTATION

What makes resisting temptation difficult, for many people, is that they don't want to discourage it completely.
Franklin P. Jones

No one knows how bad he is until he has tried to be good. There is a silly idea about that good people don't know what temptation means.
C. S. Lewis

When fleeing temptation, don't leave a forwarding address.
R. E. Phillips

Temptations, unlike opportunities, will always give you a second chance.
O. A. Battista

Opportunity knocks only once; temptation leans on the doorbell.

Nothing makes it easier to resist temptation than a proper upbringing, a sound set of values, and witnesses.
Franklin P. Jones

TENACITY

Let me tell you the secret that has led me to my goal.
My strength lies solely in my tenacity.

Louis Pasteur

TEN COMMANDMENTS

The Supreme Court has handed down the
Eleventh Commandment: "Thou shalt not, in
thy classrooms, read the first ten."

Fletcher Knebel

TERROR

The one means that wins the easiest victory
over reason: terror and force.

Adolf Hitler

TERRORIZE

No one can terrorize a whole nation unless we
are all his accomplices.

Edward R. Murrow

THANKFULNESS

Who does not thank for little will not thank for much.

If you can't be satisfied with what you have
received, be thankful for what you have escaped.

If a fellow isn't thankful for what he's got, he isn't likely
to be thankful for what he's going to get.

Frank A. Clark

THINKING

If I look confused it's because I'm thinking.

Sam Goldwyn

If everybody thought before they spoke, the silence
would be deafening.

Gerald Barzan

There is no expedient to which a man will not go to
avoid the real labor of thinking.

Thomas A. Edison

Thinking is when your mouth stays shut and your
head keeps talking to itself.

Thinking is the hardest work there is, which is
probably why so few engage in it.

Henry Ford

The probable reason some people get lost
in thought is because it is unfamiliar
territory to them.

THRIFT

Take care of your pennies and your dollars will
take care of themselves.

Take care of your pennies and your dollars will take
care of your widow's next husband.

TIME

Our greatest danger in life is in permitting the urgent things to crowd out the important.

Charles E. Humel

Time is a great healer, but a poor beautician.

Lucille S. Harper

Dost thou love life? Then do not squander time, for that is the stuff life is made of.

Benjamin Franklin

Time and tide wait for no man.

Geoffrey Chaucer

Time and tide wait for no man, but time always stands still for a woman of thirty.

Robert Frost

It is later than you think.

Lost yesterday, somewhere between sunrise and sunset, two golden hours, each set with sixty diamond minutes. No reward is offered, for they are gone forever.

Horace Mann

The person who always watches the clock will never become the man of the hour.

We never shall have any more time. We have, and we have always had, all the time there is.

Arnold Bennett

Since thou art not sure of a minute, throw
not away an hour.

Benjamin Franklin

A stitch in time saves nine.

Time flies. It's up to you to be the navigator.

Robert Orben

The right way to kill time is to work it to death.

R. G. LeTourneau

Time is
Too Slow for those who Wait,
Too Swift for those who Fear,
Too Long for those who Grieve,
Too Short for those who Rejoice,
But for those who Love
Time is not.

Henry Van Dyke

Without time, everything good and bad
would happen at once. Trouble would
worsen and joy would blur.

R. E. Phillips

TIRED

Never tell anyone they look tired; it only makes
people feel worse.

Susan Blond

TOGETHER

Alone we can so do little; together
we can do so much.

Helen Keller

TOLERANT

Always be tolerant with those who disagree
with you. After all, they have a perfect right
to their ridiculous opinions.

Nothing makes you more tolerant of a neighbor's
noisy party than being there.

TOMBSTONE

The tombstone is about the only thing that can stand
upright and lie on its face at the same time.

Mary Wilson Little

TOMORROW

Never put off till tomorrow what you can do the
day after tomorrow.

Mark Twain

Tomorrow is the most important thing in life. It
comes into us at midnight very clean. It's perfect
when it arrives and it puts itself in our hands. It
hopes we've learned something from yesterday.

John Wayne

Never put off till tomorrow what you can do today.
Lord Chesterfield

Do it tomorrow. You've made enough
mistakes for one day.
Bumper Sticker

TONGUE

A slip of the foot may be soon recovered, but
that of the tongue perhaps never.

A tongue doesn't weigh much, but
many people have trouble
holding one.

Teach your child to hold his tongue; he'll learn
fast enough to speak.
Benjamin Franklin

How oftentimes is silence the wisest of replies.

Many have fallen by the edge of the sword,
but more have fallen by the tongue.

The tongue is in a wet place and slips easily.
R. E. Phillips

Sometimes the most difficult feat of muscular
strength is just holding your tongue.

TOOL

If the only tool you have is a hammer, you tend to
see every problem as a nail.
Abraham Maslow

TRAFFIC PROBLEMS

Another way to solve the traffic problems of this
country is to pass a law that only paid-for cars be
allowed to use the highways.

Will Rogers

TRAGEDY

In the theater there is comedy and
tragedy. If the house is packed it's a comedy,
otherwise it's a tragedy.

Sol Hurok

In this world there are only two tragedies: one is not
getting what one wants, and the other is getting it.

Oscar Wilde

Tragedy warms the soul, elevates the heart, can
and ought to create heroes.

Napoleon Bonaparte

TRANSGRESSORS

The way of transgressors is hard.

The Bible

The reason the way of the transgressor is hard is
because it's so crowded.

Frank Hubbard

TREASURES

Lay not up for yourselves treasures upon earth,
where moth and rust doth corrupt, and where thieves
break through and steal.

The Bible

TRIALS

The gem cannot be polished without friction,
nor man perfected without trials.

Trying times are times for trying.

All sunshine makes a desert.

TRIUMPH

Triumph is just "umph" added to "try."

TROUBLE

When I dig another out of trouble, the hole from
which I lift him is the place where I bury my own.

I am an old man and have known a great many
troubles, but most of them never happened.

Mark Twain

We should never attempt to bear more than one kind
of trouble at once. Some people bear three kinds—
all they have had, all they have now, and all
they expect to have.

Edward Everett Hale

Troubles, like babies, grow larger by nursing.
Lady Holland

It always looks darkest just before it
gets totally black.
Charlie Brown

No one is more exasperating than the guy who can
always see the bright side of our misfortunes.

As long as you laugh at your troubles, you
may be sure that you will never run out of
something to laugh at.

Jesus spoke more about trouble and crosses
and persecution than He did about
human happiness.
W. T. Purkiser

For every ailment under the sun,
There is a remedy, or there is none;
If there be one, try to find it;
If there be none, never mind it.
Mother Goose

There are people who are always anticipating
trouble, and in this way they manage to enjoy
many sorrows that never really happen to them.
Josh Billings

There's one thing to be said for inviting trouble:
It generally accepts.
May Maloo

One reason folks get into trouble is that
trouble usually starts out being fun.

TRUST

If you want favor with both God and man, and a reputation for good judgment and common sense, then trust the Lord completely; don't ever trust yourself. In everything you do, put God first, and He will direct you and crown your efforts with success.

The Bible

Trust, like fine china, once broken can be repaired but it is never quite the same.

A mighty fortress is our God,
A bulwark never failing,
Our helper He amid the flood
Of mortal ills prevailing.

Martin Luther

I told God that I had done all that I could and that now the result was in His hands; that if this country was to be saved, it was because He so willed it! The burden rolled off my shoulders. My intense anxiety was relieved and in its place came a great trustfulness!

Abraham Lincoln.

TRUTH

Why shouldn't truth be stranger than fiction? Fiction, after all, has to make sense.

Mark Twain

There is nothing so powerful as truth—and often nothing so strange.

Daniel Webster

The best way to show that a stick is crooked is not to argue about it or to spend time denouncing it, but to lay a straight stick alongside it.

D. L. Moody

Truth has to change hands only a few times to become fiction.

Truth is always strong, no matter how weak it looks, and falsehood is always weak, no matter how strong it looks.

Phillips Brooks

Men occasionally stumble over the truth, but most of them pick themselves up and hurry off as if nothing had happened.

Winston Churchill

Just why do men lie about each other when the plain truth would be bad enough?

If you tell the truth, you don't have to remember anything.

Mark Twain

And ye shall know the truth, and the truth shall make you free.

The Bible

Truth is generally the best vindication against slander.

Abraham Lincoln

Truth often suffers more by the heat of its defenders, than from the arguments of its opposers.

William Penn

UNCERTAINTY

We live in the midst of alarms; anxiety beclouds the future; we expect some new disaster with each newspaper we read.

Abraham Lincoln

In times like these, it helps to recall that there have always been times like these.

Paul Harvey

UNDERSTAND

In my belief, you cannot deal with the most serious things in the world unless you also understand the most amusing.

Winston Churchill

UNDERSTOOD

Nothing worse could happen to one than to be completely understood.

Carl G. Jung

UNHAPPINESS

Much unhappiness results from our inability to
remember the nice things that happen to us.

W. N. Rieger

The most unhappy of all men is he who
believes himself to be so.

Hume

It's the most unhappy people who
most fear change.

Mignon McLaughlin

UNSELFISHNESS

The secret of being loved is in being lovely; and the
secret of being lovely is in being unselfish.

J. G. Holland

The wise man does not lay up treasure. The more
he gives to others, the more he has for his own.

Lao-Tse

Grief and pain are but the soil from which springs the
lovely plant—unselfishness. Be gentle and learn how
to suffer. . . . Whatever you can do to live bravely—
without impatience or repining—will help you to live
someday in joyful contentment.

Helen Keller

VACATION

A day away from some people is like a
month in the country.

Howard Dietz

No one needs a vacation so much as the
person who has just had one.

Elbert Hubbard

VALUES

The world has forgotten, in its concern with Left and
Right, that there is an Above and Below.

Glen Drake

Try not to become a man of success but rather
to become a man of value.

Albert Einstein

VANITY

Vanity is often the unseen spur.

Thackeray

Some people are so intractably vain that when they admit they are wrong they want as much credit for admitting it as if they were right.

Sydney Harris

Most of us would be far enough from vanity if we heard all the things that are said about us.

Joseph Rickaby

VARIETY

The great source of pleasure is variety.

Samuel Johnson

Variety's the very spice of life, that gives it all its flavor.

William Cowper

VICE PRESIDENT

Once there were two brothers: one ran away to sea, the other was elected vice president—and nothing was ever heard from either of them again.

Thomas Marshall

A vice president is a person who finds a molehill on his desk in the morning and must make a mountain out of it by five P.M.

Fred Allen

The man with the best job in the country is the vice president. All he has to do is get up every morning and say, "How's the president?"

Will Rogers

VICTORY

Victory goes to the player who makes the next-to-the-last mistake.

Victory is gained only through conflict.

One of the greatest victories you can gain over a man is to beat him at politeness.

VIRTUE

Virtue is to herself the best reward.

Henry Moore

VIRTUES

I place economy among the first and most important virtues, and public debt as the greatest of dangers. We must make our choice between economy and liberty, or profusion and servitude.

Thomas Jefferson

It has been my experience that folks who have no vices have very few virtues.

Abraham Lincoln

VISION

Vision is of God. A vision comes in advance
of any task well done.

Katherine Logan

VOTE

Whenever a fellow tells me he's bipartisan I know
he's going to vote against me.

Harry S. Truman

When a political columnist says "every thinking man,"
he means himself. When a candidate appeals to
"every intelligent voter," he means everybody who's
going to vote for him.

Harry Reasoner

Voter: "I wouldn't vote for you, if you were
St. Peter himself!!"
Candidate: "If I were St. Peter, you wouldn't
be in my district."

WAITING

While we keep a man waiting, he reflects
on our shortcomings.

All things come to him who waits—even justice.
Austin O'Malley

WALL STREET

It's not the bears and the bulls that make you lose
money on Wall Street. It's the bum steers.

WANTS

You can't have everything. Where would you put it?
Steven Wright

If you don't get everything you want, think of the
things you don't get that you don't want.
Oscar Wilde

WAR

I don't know what kind of weapons will be used in the third world war, assuming there will be a third world war. But I can tell you what the fourth world war will be fought with—stone clubs.

Albert Einstein

Grass never grows where my horse has trod.

Attila the Hun

In the last 3421 years of recorded history only 268 have seen no war.

Ariel and Will Durant

WASTE

Waste not, want not.

WATERMELON

When one has tasted it (watermelon) he knows what the angels eat.

Mark Twain

WEALTH

Discipline begets abundance.

Abundance, unless we use the utmost care, destroys discipline.

Don't weary yourself trying to get rich. Why waste your time? For riches can disappear as though they had the wings of a bird!

The Bible

After a rich man gets rich, his next ambition is to get richer.

WEATHER

Everybody talks about the weather but nobody does anything about it.

Mark Twain

WEIGHT

All you have to do to lose weight is mix plenty of self-control with everything you eat.

WELCOME

Don't visit your neighbor too often, or you will outwear your welcome.

The Bible

WELFARE

In these days of increasing pressure for a welfare state, it behooves us to remember that Patrick Henry did not say, "Give me security or give me death!"

John Davis Lodge

WICKED

No man ever becomes wicked all at once.

The wicked flee when no man pursueth;
but the righteous are bold as a lion.

The Bible

WIFE

A worthy wife is her husband's joy and crown;
the other kind corrodes his strength and
tears down everything he does.

The Bible

The man who finds a wife finds a good thing;
she is a blessing to him from the Lord.

The Bible

A cheerful wife is the joy of life.

The man who says his wife can't take a joke forgets
that she took him.

Man's best possession is a sympathetic wife.

Euripides

Choose a wife rather by your ear than your eye.

A prudent wife is from the Lord.

The Bible

★320★

WILL

Put your will in neutral so God can shift you.

Where there's a will there's a way.

WIN

It isn't whether you win or lose. It's how
you place the blame.

If you cannot win, make the one ahead of you
break the record.
Jan McKeithen

To win you have to risk loss.
Jean-Claude Killy

WISDOM

Never thumb your nose at a man on a rock pile.
Committing a great truth to memory is admirable;
committing it to life is wisdom.
William A. Ward

Wise men are not always silent, but know
when to be.

The fear of the Lord is the beginning of wisdom.
The Bible

Pain makes man think. Thought makes man wise.
Wisdom makes life endurable.
John Patrick

The doorstep to the temple of wisdom is a knowledge of our own ignorance.

Charles H. Spurgeon

WISE

The art of being wise is the art of knowing what to overlook.

William James

He is a wise man who does not grieve for the things which he has not, but rejoices for those which he has.

Epictetus

He that walketh with wise men shall be wise.

The Bible

The wise don't expect to find life worth living; they make it that way.

WISH

Wishes never filled the bag.

With wishing comes grieving.

What ardently we wish we soon believe.

Edward Young

Our blunders mostly come from letting our wishes interpret our duties.

A. Maclaren

WIT

After wisdom comes wit.
Evan Esar

Wit is the salt of conversation, not the food.
William Hazlitt

Brevity is the soul of wit.
William Shakespeare

Wit is the sudden marriage of ideas which
before their marriage were not perceived
to have any relationship.
Mark Twain

Wit has a deadly aim, and it is possible to prick
a large pretense with a small pin.
Marya Mannes

WOMAN

A woman can make a man feel older or
younger than his years if she so chooses.

Being a woman is a terribly difficult task since
it consists principally in dealing with men.

Women were made with a sense of humor so they
could love men instead of laughing at them.
Will Rogers

A good woman inspires a man; a brilliant woman
interests him; a beautiful woman fascinates him;
and a sympathetic woman gets him.
Helen Rowland

WORD

The difference between the right word and the almost right word is the difference between lightning and the lightning bug.

Mark Twain

A word fitly spoken is like apples of gold in pictures of silver.

The Bible

A word from the heart goes straight to the heart.

Abbe Huvelin

WORDS

Kind words are like honey—enjoyable and healthful.

The Bible

The man of few words and settled mind is wise; therefore, even a fool is thought to be wise when he is silent. It pays him to keep his mouth shut.

The Bible

Language is the dress of thought.

Samuel Johnson

Words are things; and a small drop of ink, falling like dew upon a thought, produces that which makes thousands, perhaps millions, think.

Lord Byron

Four-letter words that changed the world: love, hope, care, heal, work, feel, duty, home, good, kind, pity, rest, seek, pray, live.

All words are pegs to hang ideas on.

Henry Ward Beecher

Words are a powerful drug, and many men are
destroyed from their much use.

R. E. Phillips

It is astonishing what power words have over man.

Napoleon Bonaparte

Better one word before than two after.

WORK

To get the true measure of a man's capacity, note
how much more he does than is required of him.

The average human being in any line of work
could double his productive capacity overnight
if he began right now to do all the things he knows
he should do, and to stop doing all the things
he knows he should not do.

Elmer G. Leterman

Few men ever drop dead from overwork, but many
quietly curl up and die because of undersatisfaction.

Sydney Harris

Would you like to find out what it's like to be a
member of a minority group? Try putting in an
honest day's work occasionally.

Kelly Fordyce

For a real quick energy boost, nothing beats
having the boss walk in.

Robert Orben

The hardest thing about making a living is that you
have to do it again the next day.

I never did a day's work in my life. It was all fun.

Thomas A. Edison

Thank God every morning when you get up that you
have something to do which must be done, whether
you like it or not. Being forced to work, and forced to
do your best, will breed in you temperance,
self-control, diligence, strength of will, content, and a
hundred other virtues which the idle never know.

Charles Kingsley

By working faithful eight hours a day,
you may eventually get to be a boss
and work twelve hours a day.

Robert Frost

My father taught me to work; he did not
teach me to love it.

Abraham Lincoln

Every man's work is a portrait of himself.

The dictionary is the only place where success
comes before work.

Arthur Brisbane

There is no substitute for hard work.

Thomas A. Edison

If you would like to leave footprints in the sands of time, you had better wear work shoes.

Herbert V. Prochnow

My parents always told me that people will never know how long it takes you to do something. They will only know how well it is done.

Nancy Hanks

WORRY

Worry is a thin stream of fear trickling through the mind. If encouraged, it cuts a channel into which all other thoughts are drained.

A. S. Roche

The soil of tension and frenzy is productive of the plant of worry.

John Haggai

Worry often gives a small thing a big shadow.

Peb Jackson

We would worry less about what others think of us if we realized how seldom they do.

Ethel Barrett

Worry is interest paid on trouble before it falls due.

William Ralph Inge

Take therefore no thought for the morrow; for the morrow shall take thought for the things of itself. Sufficient unto the day is the evil thereof.

Jesus Christ

Don't cross your bridges until you come to them.

Don't cry over spilt milk.

Early in my business career I learned the folly of worrying about anything. I have always worked as hard
as I could, but when a thing went wrong and could
not be righted, I dismissed it from my mind.

Julius Rosenwald

The reason why worry kills more than work is that
more people worry than work.

Robert Frost

There are two days in the week about which
and upon which I never worry. . . . One of these
days is Yesterday. . . . And the other day I
do not worry about is Tomorrow.

Robert Jones Burdette

There is only one way to happiness and
that is to cease worrying about things which are
beyond the power of our will.

Epictetus

WORTH

A man's real worth is determined by what he does
when he has nothing to do.

WRINKLES

Wrinkles should merely indicate where
smiles have been.

Mark Twain

WRITER

Every writer is a frustrated actor who recites his lines
in the hidden auditorium of his skull.
Rod Sterling

The role of the writer is not to say what we can say,
but what we are unable to say.
Anais Nin

Many people who want to be writers don't really
want to be writers. They want to have been writers.
They wish they had a book in print.
James Michener

To hold a pen is to be at war.
Voltaire

I never desire to converse with a man who has
written more books than he has read.
Samuel Johnson

Why do writers write? Because it isn't there.
Thomas Berger

Thinking is the activity I love best, and writing is
simply thinking through my fingers.
Isaac Asimov

What no wife of a writer can ever understand is that a
writer is working when he's staring out the window.
Burton Rascoe

WRITING

If you want to change the world, pick up your pen.
Martin Luther

Writing is the hardest way of earning a living, with the possible exception of wrestling alligators.

Olin Miller

Writing is the work of a slave.

Charles H. Spurgeon

Writing a book is an adventure. To begin with, it is a toy and an amusement. Then it becomes a mistress, then it becomes a master, then it becomes a tyrant. The last phase is that just as you are about to be reconciled to your servitude, you kill the monster, and fling him to the public.

Winston Churchill

Your audience is one single reader. I have found that sometimes it helps to pick out one person—a real person you know—or an imagined person and write to that one.

John Steinbeck

The greatest part of a writer's time is spent in reading, in order to write; a man will turn over a half a library to make one book.

Samuel Johnson

There's nothing to writing. All you do is sit down at a typewriter and open a vein.

Red Smith

It helps to read the sentence aloud.

Harry Kemelman

When you catch an adjective, kill it.

Mark Twain

Write freely and as rapidly as possible and throw the whole thing on paper. Never correct or rewrite until the whole thing is down. Rewrite in process is usually found to be an excuse for not going on.

John Steinbeck

I always begin with a character or characters, and then try to think up as much action for them as possible.

John Irving

I write the ending first. Nobody reads a book to get to the middle.

Mickey Spillane

The last thing we decide in writing a book is what to put first.

Blaise Pascal

Action is character.

F. Scott Fitzgerald

You can never know enough about your characters.

W. Somerset Maugham

A good title is the title of a successful book.

Raymond Chandler

Never talk about what you are going to do until after you have written it.

Mario Puzo

Don't tell anybody what your book is about and don't show it until it's finished. It's not that anybody will steal your idea but that all that energy that goes into the writing of your story will be dissipated.

David Wallechinsky

First you're unknown, then you write one book and you move up to obscurity.
Martin Myers

Writing is easy. All you do is stare at a blank sheet of paper until drops of blood form on your forehead.
Gene Fowler

He writes so well he makes me feel like putting my quill back in my goose.
Fred Allen

Write what you like; there is no other rule.
O. Henry

WRONG

One of the hardest things in this world to do is to admit you are wrong. And nothing is more helpful in resolving a situation than its frank admission.

The remedy for wrongs is to forget them.

YAWN

A yawn is a silent shout.
G. K. Chesterton

YESTERDAY

Yesterday is a cancelled check; tomorrow is a
promissory note; today is the only cash you
have—so spend it wisely.
Kay Lyons

YOUNG

Anyone who stops learning is old, whether at twenty
or eighty. Anyone who keeps learning stays young.
The greatest thing in life is to keep your mind young.
Henry Ford

YOURSELF

"Be yourself" is about the worst advice
you can give some people.

YOUTH

We are only young once. That is all
society can stand.
Bob Bowen

Except for an occasional heart attack I feel
as young as I ever did.
Robert Benchley

I am not young enough to know everything.
James M. Baffie

Youth is a wonderful thing. What a crime
to waste it on children.
George Bernard Shaw

Rejoice, O young man, in thy youth; and let thy heart
cheer thee in the days of thy youth, and walk in the
ways of thine heart, and in the sight of thine eyes:
but know thou, that for all these things God will bring
thee into judgment. Therefore remove sorrow from
thy heart, and put away evil from thy flesh: for
childhood and youth are vanity.
The Bible

If you want to recapture your youth, just cut
off his allowance.
Al Bernstein

ZOO

When I was a kid I said to my father one afternoon, "Daddy, will you take me to the zoo?" He answered, "If the zoo wants you, let them come and get you."

Jerry Lewis

MORE from
Michael Reagan
& Bob Phillips...

Michael Reagan, one of America's premier conservative radio talk-show hosts and author of *On the Outside Looking In*, publishes a highly informative newsletter en-titled *Michael Reagan's Monthly Monitor*. This publication offers insider facts, tips, and insights on all the latest news of concern to American citizens. For more information about obtaining a subscription, write to:

> Mediafax
> 10381 Old Placerville Rd., Suite #120
> Sacramento, CA 95827-9944

Or, you can call 1-800-329-9778.

Bob Phillips, Ph.D., has written more than 30 books with combined sales of three million copies, including the new *Unofficial Liberal Joke Book*, which lampoons everything from political correctness to balancing the budget. For more information on how to purchase this or other Bob Phillips books, contact your local bookstore or send a self-addressed stamped envelope to:

> Family Services
> P.O. Box 9363
> Fresno, CA 93702